To Ollie &

lots of love

Robin ★
xx

Proto Stonehenge
in Wales

Robin Heath

Robin Heath is the author of *A Key to Stonehenge* (1993), *Sun, Moon & Stonehenge* (1998), *Sun, Moon & Earth* (1999), *Stonehenge* (2000), *The Measure of Albion (with John Michell*, 2004), *The Lost Science of Measuring the Earth* (2006), *Powerpoints* (2007), and *Bluestone Magic* (2010).

Bluestone Press
- 2014 -

ORIGINAL

12/14

Proto Stonehenge in Wales

Robin Heath

ISBN No. 978 0 95261 518 7

For further information about Bluestone Press publications, visit our website
www.skyandlandscape.com
or www.robinheath.info

Front cover artwork of Stonehenge by Suzannah Fussell,
rear cover artwork of Pentre Ifan by Ruth Barwell.
Cover design by Robin Heath.

Bluestone Press

In memory of Irene Earis, MA(Oxon),
Academic researcher, poet, and archaeoastronomer

Acknowledgements

I would like to thank all those who offered their encouragement and contributions during the research, preparation and writing of this book. In particular, helpful discussions were enjoyed with Dr Euan MacKie, John and Emma Powell, John Neal, John Spikes, Brent Brown and several local farmers whose land includes some of the sites mentioned in this book.

Prior to her untimely death in December 2013, my dear colleague, the late Irene Earis, offered her customary incisive editing comments on the first half of the text, and was fully able to see where this work was leading. My loss was immense, made worse almost immediately afterwards when a second colleague, the writer, prehistorian and landscape *guru* John Sharkey also passed away.

I want to thank my brother Richard who has been of great assistance, not only because he is so fully familar with the ancient number sciences but also because he is a published author and knows the score.

Grateful thanks are offered to Sarah Sharp for locating and then giving permission for me to reproduce the watercolour of Pentre Ifan, painted by her late mother, Ruth Barwell. The watercolour of Stonehenge on the front cover was painted by Suzannah Fussell, reproduced by kind permission.

During the production of this book, my greatest help was my wife, Tricia, whose patience is immense and who hacked through all the tedious undergrowth of spelling, grammatical and typographical mistakes and rebuked constantly my tendency to use slang terms. We have fought each other, sometimes paragraph by paragraph, in order to find the necessary compromises that a book of this size must embrace. The book would have been diminished without her hard won loving contribution.

Proto Stonehenge in Wales

Contents

Bibliography - recommended books are mentioned at the relevant
place in the narrative, by title, author, publisher and date.

Carningli summit with the dolmen Llech y Drybedd in the foreground. This peak dominates the coastal landscape between Cardigan and Fishguard, in West Wales. Much of its impressive megalithic legacy has survived the ages, and it reveals an astonishing cultural activity that took place here, around 3000 BC, one which was to provide many of the features employed in the design of Stonehenge. The photograph shows a 'mirroring' of the capstone of the dolmen with the summit of Carningli, a visual connection linking the two sites.

Standing on parade. The tallest stone at Stonehenge at 22 ft, stone 56. Its fallen companion lies at its side, and the most westerley placed Station stone, stone 93, is in the left background.

Foreword

This book is about a discovery, one that exposes an aspect of our prehistory that has since been lost to us. Almost nothing can be found of it within our history books, largely because our specialists in such matters have told us that it never happened, or that it could never have happened. Yet we will demonstrate that this activity not only happened, it once formed a crucially important technology within a culture we today still think of as being essentially barbaric.

The discovery to be described here is directly connected with the construction, between around 3100 BC and 1800 BC, of what has become adopted as Britain's national temple, Stonehenge. Like that monument, this discovery raises our perception concerning the capabilities of our Neolithic ancestors. There is more evidence left on the ground to expand on those capabilities, the narrative offering an entry into a new dimension of what some might choose to call 'Stone-Age technology'. Here, it is preferred to call it megalithic science, and its study provides a breathtaking perspective on a technology the world has forgotten, or chosen to forget, revealed in the hills of coastal West Wales which not coincidentally, is also the location of the Preseli bluestones.

During the past five or six years, almost every prehistorian archaeologist has been pounding the beat in this small and remote area of Wales. The *zeitgeist* has drawn them here and urged them to look for something, yet they have been unable to detect that something even when it has been right under their feet, and this book offers good reasons for their apparent inability to connect.

There is nothing more tasking for an author than to attempt to present a factual narrative in such a way that it can be read, comprehended and hopefully enjoyed by both academic prehistorians and non-specialist readers alike, whether or not they agree with my conclusions. The balance is hard to achieve and maintain, and in *Proto Stonehenge in Wales* I recognise that I may have fallen short of my goal. However, the whole bundle is here, the context and background to the subject, the research with all the relevant data, the discovery, the analysis and the conclusions - it's all here between the covers of a single small book which at least delivers on what the title promises. For any mistakes, omissions and other blunders, I accept full responsibility, and can therefore always be found where the buck stops.

Introduction

During the past century or so, balloons, aeroplanes and then orbiting satellites have been photographing the surface of the earth from above. Amongst the other duties required of this aerial activity, these photographs and films have transformed archaeology and led to hugely significant discoveries being made. From the air, one can see things that cannot be appreciated at ground level. The truth of this statement is nowhere better demonstrated than at Stonehenge, whose overall form cannot be appreciated by walking through or around the monument (*see photograph above*). To do that one needs an accurate plan, a model or a photograph taken from the air. Then Stonehenge reveals geometrical shapes, lots of them. Stonehenge can be appreciated as a geometrical design. There's the Aubrey circle, Sarsen circle, Station stone rectangle, Bluestone circle and Trilithon ellipse.

During the middle of the last century, the true extent and accuracy of the Nazca lines in southern Peru and their accompanying geoglyphs became recognised for the first time. Aeroplanes began to photograph a swathe of geometrical shapes on the landscape beneath. Although these had been brought to the attention of the Spanish in 1553, and had been widely studied by many people during more recent centuries, the lines and geoglyphs became a public sensation only once the aerial photographs and scratchy movie films became available. People saw what these shapes looked like, how the patterns and linearities interacted, and clamoured to find out more about these mysterious shapes and lines, and about the culture that saw fit to create these shapes around 500 AD. The site is now rightly on the UNESCO World Heritage Site list.

Spread over an area of 150 square miles between the towns of Nazca and Palpa, the Nazca shapes and lines, like Stonehenge, could not be adequately seen or evaluated from ground level, except by using modern surveying techniques and producing a plan. It appeared as though they were designed to be seen from aloft, and many archaeologists and historians have suggested that they were built to please the Gods of the people who constructed them. In the modern fashion, some popular writers proposed that they were made by passing aliens, precisely the same proposals that have been made concerning the origins of Stonehenge. It is a proposition made whenever something ancient and strange cannot be explained by the orthodox model of history, or prehistory.

This book is about a discovery made during the summer of 2013 in the far west of Wales, in north Pembrokeshire, within the curtilage of the Pembrokeshire National Park. This discovery also takes the form of a geometrical structure, and it too cannot be appreciated from ground level. Its component sites are all constructed on high ground making it impossible to see the geometry from above. But unlike the Nazca site, this site is from a much earlier age, the Neolithic, like Stonehenge but perhaps even a little earlier. Unlike the linearities on the Nazca Plain, this artifact contains within its form seriously accurate geometrical shapes and astonishingly accurate values for the length of the year and lunar month. And it was surely conceived of and designed by human brains, and built with human hands. By our ancestors.

For anyone interested in prehistory, the history of science, or the development of human thinking, this small coastal area of Wales has concealed for a long, long time a previously unrecognised megalithic artifact, as important as any, and one revealing a hugely significant component of our prehistoric past, a component that also connects it directly with Stonehenge, on Salisbury Plain. That same component has since been forgotten, lost to our history books and to the modern world.

This book will demonstrate that people who lived in Wales during the neolithic period found a way to observe, measure and then to store the major time periods of the sun and moon in order to study astronomy, integrating the apparently wayward motions of the two luminaries into an accurate and comprehensive calendar system. The artifact had been designed to measure the length of the year, month and other cosmic periods, enabling their inter-relationships to be studied year-on-year, eclipses to be predicted and tide times to be known. All this was incorporated into the building of a proto-Stonehenge, in the Preseli region of coastal West Wales. And it all still remains in place and largely intact. You may go and visit it, and using Google Earth, you can even observe it from space, measure it and confirm everything that is claimed for it in this book.

Proto Stonehenge in Wales

There is already a well-investigated and well-publicised link between this region and Stonehenge. Nearly a century ago, Dr Hubert H Thomas, a Welsh geologist, wrote up and published petrological evidence suggesting that the bluestones found at Stonehenge originated from specific outcrops in the Preseli mountains. Because these sources were so localised, Thomas's discovery led to the suggestion that the Stonehenge bluestones were taken by deliberate human intent from these outcrops along the spine of the Preselis, rather than through the action of glacial flow. Ninety years on, the wheel is still in spin on this issue and takes the form of an argument that has at times become quite acrimonious and sometimes personal.

The issue is an important one, it centres on whether or not these stones, many weighing several tons, arrived at Stonehenge by the deliberate intent of Neolithic tribesmen, or not. And if they did, why? How were they transported and what was the route taken? Seeking out further evidence to support the intentional taking of these stones to Stonehenge has become one of the most focussed searches within recent prehistoric research by archaeologists, whose chief spokesperson is presently Professor Mike Parker Pearson (UCL).

To identify a second link connecting Stonehenge with the Preseli mountains should therefore be of great topical interest to specialists and non-specialists alike. It is important at the outset to identify why such a discovery should be so significant. The mission statement of the recent archaeological research has been to use modern and improved petrological techniques to identify the exact 'fingerprint' of every one of the Stonehenge bluestones, and then to trace the precise location, wherever possible, from where each of these megaliths originated. And almost a century after Dr Thomas's original work, the answer as to whether or not the bluestones were deliberately transported to Stonehenge does appear to lie within our grasp. But then there's a big problem to face. While the importance of such a unequivocable 'proof' cannot be in any doubt, confirmation of Thomas's original theory would immediately present prehistoric archaeologists with a much more significant question: Why were the bluestones taken to Stonehenge? On this matter they presently have no convincing answers.

This book reveals evidence that provides an answer to this question, one that also greatly enlarges our perspective on the whole matter of Stonehenge. With this answer comes an explanation as to what certain parts of the monument were for, why it was built, and even why it was located where it is, on Salisbury Plain. The artifact described in this book displays unequivocal and integrated astronomical, geometrical and metrological features that are identical, and clearly related, to those found within the first constructional phase of Stonehenge, currently dated between 3150 and 2750 BC. The Welsh sites are contemporary with this period, perhaps a little earlier, and they all pre-date the arrival of the later massive stones erected at Stonehenge, the sarsen circle and its inner trilithon horseshoe. The Welsh sites are more aligned with what has been termed in an early classification of Stonehenge, Phase I and II, the earlier 'bluestone phase' at the monument.

All the sites involved in this proto-Stonehenge are intervisible with each other, and with the main bluestone outcrops in the Preseli Mountains, from where there is already clear evidence that some of the larger bluestones at Stonehenge originated. The newly discovered megalithic complex, the subject of this book, provides researchers with a second, independent and robust cultural link between the Preseli region of West Wales and Stonehenge. How the bluestones arrived at Stonehenge is entirely a separate issue from this discovery of a proto-Stonehenge in the Preselis, although the Preseli artifact certainly supports the argument that they were taken there intentionally.

For readers to identify and appreciate a Proto-Stonehenge, they must first understand something of the historical context that surrounds Stonehenge. Over the past millenium various stories have been told about this unique monument, and these need to be compared with the emerging picture, described here, of the capabilities and aspirations of the megalithic culture that once saw fit to construct this and similar huge stone structures over most of Europe. This is a new story of Stonehenge.

Robin Heath
May 2014

Stonehenge - the logo. The model displays the inner part of the monument as it may once have looked before time and human interference began to take its toll. It is the part of the monument that everyone associates as Stonehenge. However, most of the early constructions at Stonehenge took place outside of this inner sanctum of circles and ellipses. These early constructions began arriving around 3100 BC, and once comprised a six foot (2m) high bank surrounding the monument, 320 feet in diameter (97.5m), fifty-six large holes dug to lie around the perimeter of a 283 ft (86.3m) circle and a huge stone to mark the midsummer sunrise from the centre of the circle. There were many other features that today are not emphasised during a tour to the stones. These form that part of the monument that will be shown to have been developed in coastal West Wales, constructed between 3150 and 2700 BC.

Chapter One

STONEHENGE
The Context

In 1967 the prehistorian archaeologist Jacquetta Hawkes, somewhat tongue in cheek, summed up the historical context of Stonehenge rather well when she suggested that,

'Every generation has the Stonehenge it deserves, or desires.'

Although this remark is essentially true, the real truth is that every generation gets the Stonehenge that has been decided upon by those archaeologists and prehistorians who held authority on matters of heritage at the time. And anyone who thinks that Stonehenge is no longer of some cultural and even political significance should watch the footage of those running battles fought there between military police and festival goers in 1985, when the monument provided the location, the timing (summer solstice) and even the focus for the gathering conflict.

Stonehenge is therefore a rather tricky subject. As Britain's national temple, Stonehenge has played many roles within the life of the nation, from far prehistory during its lengthy 1500 year construction period, to the recent construction of the new Visitor's Centre and the closing of the old road that ran right past the ruins of what once the monument had been, what could be termed the Original Visitor's Centre.

So, one might think that every aspect of this monument had by now been scrutinised to death, fully understood, yet this is not the case at all, and certainly not with regard to the monument's function. Despite a regular onslaught of excavations, investigations and interpretations since the time of James I, and a grand parade of 'experts' undertaking these acts, whether using pick and shovel or the latest technological ground radars, the whole business has, in the words of author John Michell,

'..contributed scarcely at all to resolving the problem obviously presented by the substantial presence of megalithic monuments, the problem of why they were built.'

Megalithomania, John Michell, (Thames & Hudson, 1976)

1

Proto Stonehenge in Wales

The study of Stonehenge (and many other megalithic sites) in order to answer this deceptively simple question has been largely a history of the failure to understand the monument's function. There have been libraries of data made available on this and other sites and wheelbarrowfuls of classification, but no answer has been forthcoming to the questions: Why were these megalithic monuments built? and What were they for? Magnus Magnusson eloquently focussed in on this inability to grasp the function or essence of megalithic monuments during the opening moments of a 1970 BBC Chronicle documentary about the life and work of Professor Alexander Thom,

> "Up and down the country there are hundreds of prehistoric sites, drowning in mist and heather, as remote and incomprehensible as the men who put them there at vast expense of toil, four thousand years ago, or more. Stones in circles, stones standing in stiff-shouldered lines, marching nowhere, doing nothing. What were they for? Why should a simple primitive people scratching a living from the land go to such trouble to build these seemingly pointless monuments in the middle of nowhere? Was it simply for ritual or ceremonial purposes or..?"

Chronicle, *Cracking the Stone Age Code*, BBC 1970.

The cultural history of the studies made on Stonehenge are meanwhile much more telling, and certainly more colourful. Some archaeologists have upheld the type of public persona and its accompanying accent as if of royal extraction, and many have been flamboyant characters keen to pontificate on their opinions and proselytise their theories. Meanwhile their public has continued to hound and irritate them by repeatedly asking the question posed on the previous page by John Michell. This question has never been satisfactorily answered from within archaeology.

Those who have attempted the task from beyond and outside the assumed area of expertise of academic archaeology and its adopted model of prehistory have meanwhile been fast-tracked into membership of that famous group of eccentrics, whose contradictory theories and sundry notions about Stonehenge prompted archaeologist Richard Atkinson to once describe as,

> '..that lunatic fringe of archaeology to which Stonehenge has always acted as an irresistible magnet.'

Stonehenge, Hamish & Hamilton, 1956, p.182

A psychologist might point out that it is the vacuum created by archaeology's failure to answer this deceptively simple question concerning Stonehenge and our other Neolithic monuments that has largely spawned the large number of strange theories and legends attached to these structures. Many of the monuments that once covered the landscape of Britain have suffered centuries of destruction since Roman times, mainly at the hands of the Church. By the will of Pope Gregory the Great, the 'stone idols' were to be torn down following the issue of of a papal edict, issued in 597 AD.

The man chosen to undertake this task was St Augustine of Canterbury. His mission, elicited from Rome, was to destroy the megalithic heritage of Britain and replace the monuments with Christian shrines, over-built on their ruins prior to reconsecration. This decree was evidently not a total success, because many megalithic constructions have survived this onslaught. Increasingly, after Augustine, the remaining monuments were considered devilish, many even became named after the Devil, and the God-fearing were warned not to visit let alone congregate near these sites for fear of the dire consequences that would be bound to follow. The medieval church taught us to fear the megaliths and thereby to fear our past.

In our times, we think that no such injunctions remain in place, and that our culture is 'clever and classless and free' [from John Lennon, *Working Class Hero*]. Even if that were true, is it not strange that we remain so ignorant of the purpose(s) of these monuments, of which there are thousands still standing upright across these islands and within most of northwestern Europe? And why has the subject of archaeology been unable to answer why these monuments were built or their purpose, yet refutes any idea or theory from outside of its own ranks?

One archaeologist, perhaps the only archaeologist, who ever saw fit to spell out the likely reason to his colleagues, is Dr Euan MacKie, previously of Glasgow University. In 1972, in a film intended for his undergraduate students he gave the first public account of the reason,

> "..the archaeological profession as a whole was unable to comprehend let alone reckon with the astronomical findings of professor Thom. It follows therefore that something must be missing from the training of archaeologists that prevents them from being able to understand and then incorporate the evidence presented by Thom."

So what were these findings, and what was that "something" that was "missing from the training of archaeologists"? This question is much easier to answer. The something that is missing comes about because archaeologists are normally educated in the arts, and only rarely do they have any background in the numerical sciences. As such archaeology has traditionally remained essentially a non-scientific discipline.

MacKie had observed that the single most effective attempt at answering that question about why the monuments were there and what they were for was, during the 1960s, the research of Professor Alexander Thom, the recently retired Head of Engineering at Oxford and a man with an outstanding *curriculum vitae*. Thom was exceptionally well versed in the numerical sciences, and not surprisingly, when he

began to find astronomical, geometrical and metrological qualities within stone rings, rows and other megalithic forms, he reported his findings and concluded that these qualities had formed a significant component of the culture that had erected them. This was a radical view at the time. Due to the required mathematical content in Thom's analyses, most archaeologists were incapable of making a judgement on this unexpected new source of data, and this stopped most of them from engaging with Thom's evidence, although it did not stop many of them from rejecting and criticising it.

Dr Euan MacKie

Thom was accused of being a fantasist, of projecting his scientific world-view back in time onto the megalithic monuments. If this logic were true, it hardly needs to be said that for most of archaeology's chequered history, prehistorians have equally been projecting their non-scientific world-view onto these same monuments, and in that act they have demonstrably failed to understand them. If these monuments do

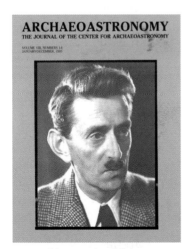

indeed contain astronomical, geometrical and metrological patterns within their structures, then it is a logical conclusion that the numerical sciences will need to be employed in order to recognise and evaluate these qualities. The projection of a scientific world-view back in time is precisely what will be needed.

The Accurate Surveying of Stone Rings

Thom had no preconceived agenda concerning stone circles when, in 1934, he began a long personal research project to survey as many of them as he could. He started, in his own words, with "a clean sheet of paper". He rapidly discovered that astronomy, measure, number and geometry played a crucial role in the design of many of the circles and stone

Alexander Thom

rows. No longer could these stone rings be described as 'rough ovoids' or 'poorly defined', often more a description of the appalling quality of many of the extant archaeological plans than of the original build quality of the stone ring. Through measurements and surveys undertaken to the highest professional standards, using theodolites and temperature corrected measuring tapes, Thom drew up very precise plans, from which he discovered that there were families of stone rings all conforming to the same geometrical rules.

These geometries were to be found at sites throughout the land, and later they were identified at sites in Ireland and Brittany. Astonishingly, archaeologists had previously not recognised these properties, and increasingly they became resentful of someone from outside their profession revealing such things. While many archaeologists were only too happy to applaud Thom's high skills in surveying and to acknowledge the accuracy of his survey plans of megalithic sites, his findings became increasingly criticised, derided and finally ignored altogether.

But Thom, an inquiring academic engineer/scientist, did not finish there. Having revealed the geometrical nature of many of the non-circular stone rings he increasingly turned his attentions to attempting to find out if their builders had been using a recogniseable unit of length. Having already recognised that his critics would demand a statistical treatment of the data, he amassed huge amounts of measurements on site, and roped in several of the sixties' leading statisticians to help develop a model from which he might present his data. Two statistical methods were designed for the purpose, one by Dr Simon Broadbent, a Cambridge statistician, and another by Professor John Hammersley, who held the post of *Readership in the Design and Analysis of Scientific Experiment* at Oxford. The initial outcome from these methods of analysis was the emergence of a unit of length of 2.720 feet ± 0.003 feet (0.8290m) that Thom called the megalithic yard.

Following later surveys at Avebury, Stonehenge and at some sites in Brittany, Thom was able to refine this measurement slightly, and in 1976 he amended the value of the megalithic yard to 2.722 feet (0.8296m). This figure was published in *Megalithic Remains in Britain and Brittany* (OUP, 1979). A tiny change, twenty-four thousandths of one inch in just over thirty-two and a half inches, it nevertheless becomes significant over long distances and even at large megalithic sites (*see appendix 4, page 101*).

Thom fought a long and gruelling battle trying to convince archaeologists of the reality of the megalithic yard, a battle he had lost by 1980. If the geometry of the stone rings had irritated archaeologists, the megalithic yard became like a red rag to a bull (*see appendix 5*).

A Historical Problem with Metrology

In the 1960s it was not easy to understand historic metrology. It had been nearly a hundred years since the subject had been abandoned by the same two nations, Britain and France, who had strived so hard to understand it during the previous two centuries. The only readily available semi-academic textbook on the subject was Arthur Berriman's *Historic Metrology* (Dent, 1953) and metrologist John Neal has subsequently shown this book to contain widespread errors, in part owing to Berriman's misunderstanding of the quantum nature of the ancient system of metrology. Quanta easily disappear in a fog of different lengths when averaging is applied to lengths taken from ancient monuments and artifacts. (See Neal, *All Done with Mirrors*, Secret Academy Press, 2000).

Thom, who had a copy of Berriman's book, knew no better than its author. Metrologically, the megalithic yard should have been named a megalithic step, the step always being a unit of two and a half times the length of its root or radix foot. In the case of the megalithic yard this root foot was the Belgic or 'Drusian' foot, fractionally related to the 'English' foot by the ratio 15:14, and whose standard canonical value is 1.088 feet (*see Neal, op cit*). Two steps make up a pace, which was Thom's eponymous 'megalithic fathom' of 5.443 feet, while his 'megalithic rod', of length 6.804 feet, is two and half times the megalithic step (*see appendix four for more information concerning the derivation of the megalithic yard*).

Astronomical Alignments at Megalithic Sites

As Thom visited sites up and down the British Isles he also investigated the astronomical properties of megalithic monuments. His surveys took account of the local horizon, and he had noticed that, from Callanish to Cornwall, many sites were located such that a notch, a mountain slope or sometimes a standing stone would mark where a solstitial or equinoctal sunrise or sunset occurred. Thom built up a large catalogue of sites that displayed a good alignment to these horizon foresights at the time the archaeologists thought that these monuments had been constructed.

However, during the 1960s the dates of many monuments were being constantly pushed back in time following application of the newly developed radiocarbon dating techniques. Because the angle of tilt of the earth's axis has been gradually reducing since the Neolithic, what was once a precision alignment later became a rather less convincing orientation, up to one degree 'out' for some moon alignments in Northern Britain, due to the change in the 'obliquity of the ecliptic', as astronomers refer to this phenomenon. Thom did not always have access to the correct date for the erection of the monuments he was assessing. In this he was not alone, all prehistorians in the 1960s were aiming at a rapidly moving target when it came to dating artifacts from the Neolithic period. There were a few very red faces to be seen amongst their ranks during the 1960s.

Recognised as a first-rate astronomer, it was supremely ironic that Thom knew all about the change in the earth's obliquity, and even knew the formula by which it could be accounted for. But for that formula to work he had to know the correct date of construction for a supposed alignment, information often erroneous, based on incorrect archaeological opinion.

During the mid-60s when Thom expanded his investigations to include the moon, he was given, in good faith, the best estimates for the construction dates of what he thought were megalithic 'lunar' observatories, but unable to identify some alignments because the dating information was incorrect. A Fellow of the Royal Astronomical Society, in 1915 Thom had calculated a comet's path and corrected official estimates of its trajectory around the sun, receiving acknowledgement of that fact with grateful thanks from the Imperial Russian Astronomer Royal.

Thom was by no means without his limitations, and possessed a quality almost ubiquitous within his generation – he was a reductionist through and through, with the mind of a Victorian scientist. He never really sought to integrate the three strands of astronomy, geometry and metrology that had been the main concerns of his work. Had he done so, then this book, or a scientific paper quite like it, could have been written up, done and dusted, fifty years ago.

While his ultra-scientific methodology provided a vital analytical technique for Thom, he never quite synthesised the astronomical, geometrical or metrological evidence in the manner the megalith builders will be shown to have done. It has been my experience that unless these three disciplines are merged together, megalithic sites do not and often cannot reveal their innermost secrets. Thom did however recognise that the combination of the three disciplines of astronomy, geometry and metrology, when applied to megalithic monments, should properly be named *megalithic science*. To orthodox historians, juxtaposing these two words created a completely perfect oxymoron. Such a thing simply could not exist.

The Sixties arrive on Archaeology's Doorstep

Thom's first book, *Megalithic Sites in Britain*, (OUP, 1967) entered the public domain in 1967, when it was described by one reviewer as,

'a well constructed parcel bomb dropped though the letter box of archaeology'.

It appeared that the profession had been caught napping, had missed the bus, and over the next decade prehistoric archaeologists became more and more disgruntled about all matters to do with archaeoastronomy and especially Alexander Thom. For a prehistorian, the 1960s were offering them quite enough things that were going bump in the night without Thom's unwelcome contribution.

Archaeologist Glyn Daniel pompously declared on the 1970 BBC Chronicle documentary on Thom's work that,

"all professional archaeologists are constantly beset by the lunatic fringe",

and then gave Thom the green light by declaring that,

"Professor Thom is not part of this",

Dr Glyn Daniel

Although Daniel was one of the facilitators of the BBC *Chronicle* documentary on Thom's findings, he was later to turn vehemently against Thom when his conclusions increasingly failed to match the archaeological model in vogue. Daniel was, at the time, the editor of *Antiquity*, the foremost UK academic journal for archaeology, and his increasingly derisory polemics led to Thom being discouraged from the highest levels of the archaeological establishment.

John Michell and the Rise of Alternative History

If the archaeologists were irritated by Thom's *Megalithic Sites in Britain*, they became positively incandescent two years later when John Michell published *The View over Atlantis* (Garnstone Press, 1969). Riding on the frothy surf of the sixties' New-Age wave and a revival in popular interest in Alfred Watkins' alignments or leys, old-Etonian Michell was a well-studied scholar and an erudite man who exposed the existence of an ancient philosophy that had once driven civilisation, claiming this was where many of the roots of our history lay.

Unlike Thom, Michell did not feel any need to appeal to the archaeologists for acceptance when they inevitably rejected his work. Largely because of this Michell managed to achieve one very important thing in this book that Thom was unable to do, he made many issues relating to Britain's distant past much clearer for the general public, and they loved him for it. He was also a very good writer, and the book sold out. *The View over Atlantis* was one of the first New Age bestsellers.

If the title alone was highly provocative and guaranteed to upset the academic establishment of the late 1960s then Michell's vision of an alternative prehistory was so removed from the current model of prehistory that many archaeologists immediately wrote lengthy letters of complaint to each other, the press, his publisher and even Michell himself, which had the effect, in Michell's words, "of a gnat on an elephant's back".

'Only within recent years, since the development of universal communications allowed us to compare the antiquities of our own countries with those of others, have we been able to see the extent of the vast ruin within which we all live. If we ignore all alterations to the landscape arising within the last three thousand years and consider the world as it must have looked in prehistoric times, the pattern that emerges is one so incompatible with our idea of civilization that it is easy to miss its significance. For what we find is this.

A great scientific instrument lies sprawled over the entire surface of the globe. At some period...almost every corner of the world was visited by a group of men who came with a particular task to accomplish. With the help of some remarkable power, by which they could cut and raise enormous blocks of stone, these men erected vast astronomical instruments, circles of erect pillars, pyramids, underground tunnels, cyclopean stone platforms, all linked together by a network of tracks and alignments, whose course from horizon to horizon was marked by stones, mounds and earthworks.'

The View Over Atlantis, John Michell, Garnstone Press, 1969, p69.

Michell once showed me some press cuttings and sundry comments he had received from archaeologists, who begged to differ with this assessment of prehistory. Some were abusive in nature. Ever the gentleman, Michell ignored the *brouhaha* caused by his book and, luckily for the rest of us, carried on writing an astonishing output of well researched books, almost none of which can be found within miles of a university library!

Thom fared rather less well. His were ground-breaking books alright, but they were not for popular consumption, unlike his lectures, which were often sell-outs. Thom's books were undergraduate textbooks, aimed only at the serious student. And as the attacks and insults about his work became more and more personal, in the late 1970's, Thom, in his mid-eighties, gradually retired from the scene. By then partially sighted, circumstances forced him to withdraw entirely from the field of battle. Despite his infirmity, he still managed to coordinate the publication of a late work which included his surveys in Brittany, *Megalithic Remains in Britain and Brittany* (OUP,1979), aided by his son Dr Archibald Thom.

A Chair in Archaeoastronomy

Thom died in 1985, aged 91. His heir apparent, Dr Clive Ruggles picked up the Thom legacy, and in 1996 was elected to the new Chair of Archaeoastronomy at the University of Leicester. On his Leicester website, Ruggles defined archaeoastronomy as,

> '...the study of beliefs and practices relating to the sky in the past, especially in prehistory, and the uses to which people's knowledge of the skies was put.'

The trap into which Ruggles fell was that his denial of precision astronomy in prehistoric Europe led automatically to rendering unimportant two of the essential other sources of valuable evidence that support precision astronomy – geometry and metrology. A leading archaeological metrologist, Professor Livio Stecchini, identified the roots of metrology as having derived from time measurements of the orbital periods of the sun, moon and planets. One would therefore surely include the use and development of metrology and geometry under the 'practices relating to the sky'. Perhaps because Ruggles never endorsed the case for precision astronomical alignments, a metrology deriving from the accurate recording of recurrent time cycles would have been seen as better left alone. Only a third of the available evidence on the subject is considered important – the astronomy - and even this, in Ruggles's world, was refuted if it claimed to involve precision astronomy (*appendix five*).

In 2013, at 61 years of age, Ruggles became professor emeritus and the course at Leicester is no longer mentioned on the university's website. Despite sterling efforts elsewhere to encourage wider interest in the subject, a decrease in interest in archaeoastronomy over recent years has led to the course at Leicester being wound up. There is currently nowhere within the UK where one can study or take any kind of qualification in archaeoastronomy, a subject which within its brief must, in the author's experience, include geometry and metrology. These three subjects are nowhere to be found linked within any archaeological curriculum, vindicating the earlier quote from Euan MacKie. The present situation is the major stumbling block for anyone who wants to attempt an answer from within academia to the question: *Why the megaliths?*

This void also exposes the single biggest reason why recent work at Stonehenge and other major sites has seen no major archaeological output incorporating any of these three subjects. Until this situation is rectified, no mainstream archaeologist can or will be able to see the cultural message that underpins the purpose for which Stonehenge was constructed, its purpose.

This is the principal reason why there has been no educational material on this aspect of the monument on display at Stonehenge, and why there have been no documentaries that discuss these aspects of Stonehenge. The inevitable consequence of this omission is that documentaries about Stonehenge add nothing beyond the overworked monument's solstitial axis, how bluestones might have healing properties, or the matter of how the bluestones might have arrived on Salisbury Plain.

The World Heritage Site Consultation Draft for Stonehenge

In 1999, a firm of consultants, Chris Blandford Associates, was hired by English Heritage to assess the requirements for a long-term management plan for Stonehenge into the twenty-first century. The result was a two hundred page Consultation Draft. Stonehenge and Avebury were identified in the preface as the two most important prehistoric landscapes in Britain, this having been decided under the UNESCO World Heritage Convention. Out of all its pages, in a single paragraph (2.4.12) within the 107 pages of the Consultation Draft, one may read that,

'While theories about the reasons for its construction, the manner of its use and its role as a sacred place abound, these can be but speculation'.

This is the nub of the matter, how it has always been for alternative perspectives other than the current archaeological model of Stonehenge, in fashion at the time. It says that the other theories, beyond those determined by archaeologists which, by implication, are to be understood as 'facts', are not worth bothering about, so because the establishment doesn't give them any thought, neither should you. They are 'but speculation'.

The Theories keep on Abounding

In view of this statement it is perhaps surprising that most of the theories that have abounded since this Consultation Draft was published have come not from the lunatic fringe, but from professional archaeologists. Timothy Darvill and Geoffrey Wainwright's 'healing stones' theory purported to answer why the bluestones were so attractive to the Wessex chieftains that they imported bluestones from West Wales to Stonehenge. Allegedly they held magical properties. Evidence for this claim was thin to say the least, and despite 'seven years field-work' in the Preseli region their work did not contribute at all to answering the principal question as to why Stonehenge was built where it is, nor for what purpose was it built, other than perhaps to provide the Wessex chieftains with a health spa or offer an A&E department to passing travellers on Salisbury Plain.

The begged question is, if the bluestones promoted such health in neolithic humans, why did the Wessex tribes not migrate *en masse* to the Preseli Hills, where surely they would have found (almost) eternal well-being, the area being littered with all shapes and sizes of bluestone megaliths?

Stonehenge and particularly the question about the source of the bluestones has attracted the attention of the leading prehistoric archaeologist of the day, Prof Mike Parker Pearson. The bluestones Welsh connection with Stonehenge is an aspect of the monument that can be dated back to Elizabethan times, and geologist George Owen's comparison of the stones at Pentre Ifan with those he had seen at Stonehenge.

> *'The stone called Maen y Gromlech upon Pentre Ifan land .. (is).. a huge and massive stone mounted on high and set on the tops of three other high stones pitched standing upright in the ground. It far surpasses for bigness and height… any other that I ever saw, saving some at Stonehenge.'*

This remark, made in 1603, came from a famous Pembrokeshire nobleman, described on a brass plaque in Nevern church as 'The Patriarch of English Geologists'. Owen's remark is the first known historical mention of Stonehenge having a possible connection with West Wales or bluestones, for almost all of the stones at and around Pentre Ifan are bluestones. The semi-legendary Merlin's earlier story that the Stonehenge stones arrived from Ireland seems historically unlikely until one discovers that the magician was allegedly born in Carmarthen (CaerMyrddin), then an Irish Diese colony, and where the main spoken language was Irish. But Merlin was surely referring to the giant sarsen stones rather than the diminutive bluestones and nobody now argues where these monsters came from – Fyfield Down, just to the east of Avebury, some 17 miles north of Stonehenge. When a geologist makes a comparison of two stone monuments he assesses it with different eyes than would a casual visitor. George Owen would surely have recognised the same stone types at both sites and his remark may have provided the cue that spurred geologist Dr H Thomas's 1923 paper on the provenance of the Stonehenge bluestones.

Thomas's petrological analyses were first published in 1923 where he identified the outcrops around Carn Menyn as the major source of these enigmatic megaliths, suggesting they had been transported to Stonehenge by human intent, rather than by glacial action. The ensuing argument as to how these stones arrived at Stonehenge still rattles on, often acrimoniously, some ninety years later. Perhaps because of this, Parker Pearson has been drawn to attempt to discover more information about the sources of the bluestones within the Preselis. This work is evidence led and of great interest, and Parker Pearson presents it extremely well, but ultimately it too does not answer the central question. It is to be hoped that one outcome of Parker Pearson's work will be to provide a definitive answer as to how the bluestones arrived at Stonehenge, which would then compliment this work, which provides a convincing suggestion as to why the bluestones might have been incorporated within the structure of Stonehenge.

Dental analyses recently undertaken on skeletons found at and near Stonehenge have revealed an apparent truth of considerable importance. An analysis on the teeth of one man revealed him to have made frequent long distance journeys between Wales and Stonehenge. Work on dental samples from other skeletons have suggested that travel took place between southern Europe and Stonehenge, possibly from Switzerland. Stonehenge as a megalithic Rolex is not too far from the astronomical theories of Gerald Hawkins (*see later*), who did present the monument as a giant cosmic clock. Stonehenge as the Original Visitor's Centre for European tourists would confirm how little has changed over the millenia, but it still leaves unanswered that pressing question as to why Stonehenge was built where it is.

The Top Five Theories about Stonehenge

Despite these novel ideas, the archaeological model of Stonehenge remains much as it was forty years ago. Type 'Stonehenge theories' into a search engine and the *New Scientist* website lists these as their top five,

A Place for the Dead (Mike Parker Pearson, Sheffield and UCL)

A Place of Healing (Timothy Darvil and Geoffrey Wainwright)

An **Astronomical Observatory** (Solstices only allowed)

Moon Worship (Lionel Sims, UEL)

UFO Landing Site (Various sources)

Three of these five 'top theories' have emerged since the Consultation Draft referred to earlier, so there appears to be no stopping abounding theories. It is well over three centuries since the rediscovery of Stonehenge's solstitial axis, which dates back to the time of William Stukely, during the middle eighteenth century. The mechanism by which the 56 Aubrey circle holes could have been used to predict solar and lunar eclipses was first mooted in the mid 1960s by the astronomer Professor Sir Fred Hoyle in response to Dr Glyn Daniel, the editor of *Antiquity*, asking him to review Dr Gerald Hawkins' book *Stonehenge Decoded* (Doubleday & Co, 1965). According to Hoyle's reply, the book was an outstanding contribution to understanding the monument. This was not at all the reply Daniel had been hoping for!

Hawkins' bestselling book about the astronomy of Stonehenge was the first to employ computer analysis, and it elicited more outrage and vitriol and more rarely heard and endangered adjectives meaning rubbish from archaeologists than could ever have been thought possible. However, it was the remarkable success of Hawkins' book that prompted Thom to write up his notes from thirty-five years of private research and publish them two years later. Poor Thom, this was a shocking case of bad timing, like pouring petrol on an already raging fire.

The moon worship theory is badly named. Astronomically based, it demonstrates how the motions of the both sun and moon could have been integrated within the structure of Stonehenge. Sims is an anthropologist at UEL and his theory can be used to explain aspects of a supposed transition from a matriarchal hunter/gatherer society (lunar) to the merging patriarchy of a Neolithic farming and trading community (solar). His idea assumes a cultural importance attached to a very transient astronomical event – a once every 18.6 years minor midwinter moonset seen from one small area on the Stonehenge Avenue by the Heel stone looking southwest during a few midwinter sunsets. The resulting setting dark moon would not even be visible during the event.

A media documentary about Dr Lionel Sims' theory unfortunately did not adequately explain his theory, and displayed an astronomically flawed explanation of the motions of the sun and moon. Sims' website article (*sims stonehenge*) does much better.

The Importance of Accurate Measurement of Angles and Lengths

None of these theories contain any reference to the geometrical and metrological design of Stonehenge despite the monument providing an abundant source of objective evidence in that regard, evidence available without digging anything up, such is the nature of what is a completely non-invasive form of prehistoric research.

Direction (angles and orientation) and distance (length) both have meaning, they are just as much part of the classification of monuments within their landscape as are construction dates, the artifacts found under and around the monument and the materials used to construct the structure itself. Such classification may appear nowhere near as exciting as the discovery of a pottery bowl or a human skull from the layers of prehistory, but this view needs to be revised.

Measurements of angles and lengths reveal a great deal of information concerning how the builders of monuments thought and what they were capable of achieving, especially if these measurements can be shown to be very accurate. Heath's first paradoxical law is: It requires the invention, development and use of precision instruments to establish whether a prehistoric monument was built as a precision instrument by a previous culture. Whether or not precision could have been built into the monument or even understood by 'chieftains' or 'astronomer-priests' within the Wessex culture remains very unclear within the present archaeological model of prehistoric Britain. The precision is doubted or refuted, although this cannot any longer be taken seriously by anyone who has seriously studied the physical layout of the monument.

This issue could have been sorted out very easily, all that was required was a decent site plan, made from an accurate survey. It is astonishing that a decent plan for the whole of the Stonehenge site only became available in 1973. Why did it take so long? Inigo Jones, the King's architect, drew up his plan in 1725 upon which he imposed the influence of classical architecture, and thereby massively distorted the monument to the point where, however much it may have pleased the King, the plan was historically useless.

Sir William Flinders Petrie undertook two accurate surveys of the larger stones of the monument in the mid 1870s, before reaching the age of twenty. He was the first to discover that the inner diameter of the sarsen circle was 100 'Cyclopean' feet, now known as 100 'geographic' Roman feet of length equal to 0.973 (English) ft. An excellent surveyor, presently available popular editions of his plans and notes fail to do justice to his abilities, and contain many blurred and distorted images, rendering impossible the recovery of either accurate dimensions or angles. His accurate plans were superceded by Thom's 1973 survey, of which more details follow.

Michell's Lintel Metrology

As an example to show what can happen when a decent plan is available, using Petrie's value for the inner diameter of the sarsen circle, John Michell convincingly showed that the width of the sarsen circle lintels is based on another known unit of length - the 'geographical' value of an 'Egyptian' Royal cubit – 1.737 feet. The inner diameter of the sarsen circle is 56 and the outer diameter is 60 of these units. [see also Heath, *Stonehenge*, 2000.] This reveals a numerical connection between the Aubrey and Sarsen circles, the former having 56 markers around its perimeter and the Sarsen circle once having had thirty uprights holding thirty lintels aloft. The numerical interplay here is essentially between the numbers 14 and 15, and Michell's discovery is metrological gold to researchers into megalithic science, as later chapters will reveal.

Because it has been the fashion to ignore metrological evidence, it is simply not true to state that there is no metrological significance to the key features at Stonehenge, nor to gloss over the obvious geometry displayed

Stonehenge means 'hanging stone'. The art of hanging stones can also be seen in the design of the dolmen, which is essentially a proto Stonehenge, and similarly creates a hard to ignore statement on the landscape, a marker for all to see, reflecting the ingenuity and power of those that built it. Shown above is Pentre Ifan, the magnificent portal grave and the centrepiece of Neolithic architecture near Newport, in the Preseli region of West Wales. The huge capstone was lifted or dragged into place aloft the uprights that still support its huge mass, and this impressive feat creates a trilithon of sorts, and represents an earlier version of the trilithons at Stonehenge (*compare this monument with the illustration opposite from a well-worn 1916 edition of a popular book about the monument from the days when it cost only a shilling (5p) to walk amongst the stones*).

by these features. It is highly inconvenient within the present model of prehistory for someone to discover familiar units of length from classical antiquity incorporated within megalithic structures, because it suggests a prehistoric origin for both these units and the system of metrology.

This prologue places the reader within the present social context surrounding Stonehenge. Up to a million visitors a year bring in an estimated £93 million to English tourism. The new Visitor's Centre has recently opened, and with it begins a new era in how to tell the story of Stonehenge. It is clear that there are many stories still to be told concerning this astonishing and unique monument. Also true is that until those principal questions are addressed and answers found, then room has always to be made available for one more theory to abound, especially if it might offer an answer as to why the monument sits there on Salisbury Plain and/or what function it once served to the community that built it 'at vast expense of toil' in distant antiquity.

That is precisely what the following chapters claim to provide, through research and evidence that brings a new perspective regarding the original purpose and role of Stonehenge.

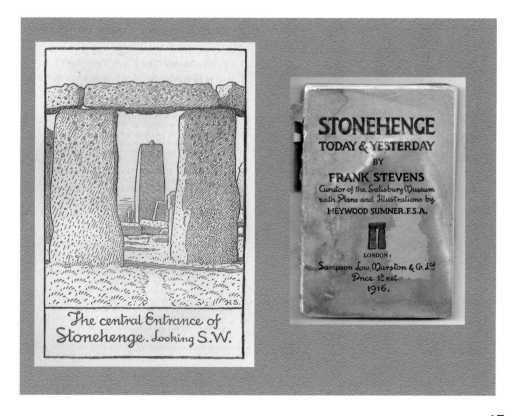

The central Entrance of Stonehenge. looking S.W.

STONEHENGE
TODAY & YESTERDAY
BY
FRANK STEVENS
Curator of the Salisbury Museum
with Plans and Illustrations by
HEYWOOD SUMNER. F.S.A.

LONDON:
Sampson Low, Marston & Co. Ltd
Price 1s net
1916.

Stonehenge
as it probably was. Plan & Bird's eye View.

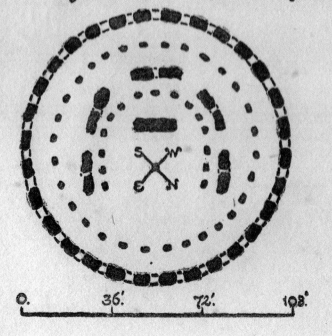

0.   36'.   72'.   108°

Chapter Two

STONEHENGE
The Hardware

In order to be able to identify a Proto-Stonehenge, one first must investigate and understand thoroughly the nature and origins of Stonehenge itself. This need no longer be a vague and obscure task, as no other megalithic monument in the world has had as much attention lavished on it over the past four centuries, nor as many books written about it, as has that magnificent ruin standing defiantly on Salisbury Plain. Unfortunately, the unique structure of huge sarsen stones that the public associate with Stonehenge (*see opposite*), its logo, represents only a small part of the story of Stonehenge, albeit very impressive, and represents the later period of construction on a site that has presented archaeological evidence that dates the location back into the mesolithic period.

The Car-Park Postholes

This most unattractively named feature is a fairly modern surprise in the history of our understanding of Stonehenge. The discovery of three substantial post-holes while excavating the car-park of the now defunct Visitor's Centre has provided the oldest known feature on the site, for the wooden remains in these holes were dated thousands of years earlier than anything else, between 8500 and 7650 BC, making them mesolithic within the modern classification of British prehistory.

Their locations were marked by a row of large concrete circles painted white onto the main surface of the car-park, and they have always remained enigmatic and controversial, although the posts must have made a most impressive visual structure when in place. The white circles can be seen using Google Earth. From the centre of the (much, much later) henge created within the ditch and bank where the stone monument we now call Stonehenge was erected some three millenia later, these post holes lie at distances of about 800 feet from the monument's centre (*see appendix two*). Whether deliberate or not, the three huge posts that once stood in these holes were placed in the direction of the most northerly moonset in the moon's 18.6 year cycle of rises and sets, viewed from along two stones that formed the southernmost longer side of the Station stone rectangle, a major feature of the early henge site discussed further in a later section.

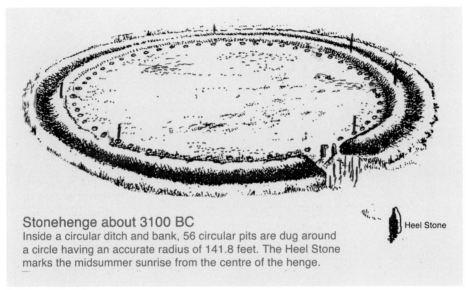

Stonehenge about 3100 BC
Inside a circular ditch and bank, 56 circular pits are dug around a circle having an accurate radius of 141.8 feet. The Heel Stone marks the midsummer sunrise from the centre of the henge.

Heel Stone

The Circular Ditch and Bank

The construction of the circular henge is now thought to have begun between 3150 and 2950 BC, and the digging of the ditch provided the chalky subsoil for making a 2 metre high circular bank, heaped up inside the circular ditch. Two entrances into the henge were constructed, one directly in the southernmost part of the bank of the henge and the other oriented in the direction of the most northerly sunrise, at the summer solstice, viewed from the henge centre, roughly 49 degrees east of true north.

Whilst it might be argued by some to be a coincidence, calculations undertaken on these two earliest features on the site show them to mark the two most northerly setting places of the sun and moon, the former each year at the summer solstice, and the latter every 18.6 years at the major standstill of the moon. The only assumption that has to be made is that those posts placed in the car-park post-holes once rose about twenty feet above the ground and may once have formed some kind of gantry, acting as an artificial horizon. (*JHA*, Thom family, Stonehenge, Vol 5, (1974), p89). Although it is tempting to speculate that these posts held lintels, making them a proto-Stonehenge from 8000 BC, there is no evidence to support this, and neither would lintels have been necessary to make the required observations of the most northerly setting moon at the major standstill.

The Heel stone

The first stone to be deliberately placed on the present Stonehenge site and to have survived until today was a very large sarsen stone megalith, now referred to as the Heel stone. Its placement on site is presently dated from between 3000 BC and 2800 BC. A rough and irregular stone, sixteen feet high and leaning back towards the monument, it is thought to have been erected contemporaneously with the construction of what is now called the Aubrey circle (about which more later), after the seventeenth century antiquarian John Aubrey.

The Heel stone was once one of a pair, its companion stone placed a few feet to the north, such that the pair were perpendicular to the axis of symmetry of the emerging monument. Today, only its post-hole remains. These two stones formed a portal, aligned such that the midsummer sunrise shone through the gap between them. A second pair of stones was similarly aligned across the axis, within the boundary of the Aubrey circle, both pairs once acting as would sights on a rifle barrel to accurately aim at and thus reinforce the importance of the midsummer sunrise axis of the monument, when viewed from the centre of the henge. Walking to the monument from the northeast towards the Heel stone, these portals would also be oriented towards the setting midwinter sun.

Of this second pair of stones only one still remains on the site, also a very large rough stone, now recumbent, once called the Slaughtering stone on account of the reddish staining on the sarsen sandstone from which it is comprised.

An Astronomical Function for the Heel stone

Today, almost every citizen of planet earth knows that the midsummer sun will rise over the Heel stone, which it still does, more or less. But because the earth's tilt angle has reduced since 3000 BC, the sunrise takes place nearly a degree to the right of where it originally did. On the occasion of the morning of the summer solstice, tens of thousands of people gather at Stonehenge to observe a magical moment, just after 4.00 am, when the ascending sun clips the Heel stone, if it is not cloudy. The news media invariably report on the event, sometimes, with photographic proof of the event. In truth the sunrise occurs well to the left of the Heel stone, the sun once rose in the gap between the Heel stone and an adjacent stone.

The legend behind the current name of this stone is itself a stored piece of astronomical information. The legend says that the tolerably convincing footprint mark set deep into the stone was made when the Devil threw the stone at a passing friar who had witnessed that the mysterious stone had been erected by Old Nick himself. Running off in the opposite direction the stone caught the monk on his heel. This unlikely folk tale is a yarn that helped the medieval Church instil fear concerning the pagan origins of this huge standing stone, hence its name of the Friar's Heel Stone. In ancient British (the language of Britain before the Anglo-Saxon conquests) 'friar heel' would have been understood by pronunciation as 'appearance of the sun'. Later written Welsh would have *Ffrîw yr Haul*, which does reveal the origin of the name of this stone (the Greek word *Helios* also means sun).

This source is not based on any text from ancient times, and has nothing to do with any stone-throwing Devil, yet it suggests the function of the stone - to mark the appearance of the sunrise. But which sunrise? For that answer one would have to know the right time to be standing in the centre of Stonehenge with one's back to the highest trilithon, looking through the widest portal in the sarsen circle. This would be the summer solstice. But it is also true that walking towards Stonehenge at sunset on the winter solstice would present the sunset shining through the aligned gaps in the portal stones of which the Heel stone and the Slaughter stone are the remaining examples.

The hidden information hidden within the Friar's Heel legend would be Stonehenge/sunrise/this stone, and it tells those that understand the legend that it is the relationship between the midsummer rising sun and the Heel stone that was still understood during early Christian times, when there were indeed large numbers of friars available and being encouraged to spot the Devil transporting large upright stones, as since the Council of Tours in 657 AD it became a serious offence to worship such stones. It was probably then that the meaning of the stone's earlier function, as a solstice marker, would have been adapted to serve the post-Augustine anti-pagan mission of the Church.

The true meaning of this hoary legend could only reveal itself to somebody who understood Welsh (the language of the tribe), had an interest in the folklore associated with megalithic sites (the folklorist) and understood astronomy (the archaeoastronomer). Archaeoastronomy is currently not taught in any UK university, folklore is not widely valued as an archaeological resource, and the Welsh language is spoken by less than a million people in Britain. Yet despite all these barriers, the message still managed to emerge into the sunlight at the beginning of the 21st century!

The Aubrey Circle

The Aubrey circle comprised fifty-six large pits, dug into the chalk. Averaging 0.7m deep and over a metre in diameter, each hole was neatly dug on the perimeter of an accurate circle on a constant radius struck from the centre of the henge. It remains popular to assume that large posts were placed in each hole, only to be removed within a 'short period of time', this varying between 60 and 250 years depending on which archaeological book one refers to. One of the earliest features at the Stonehenge site, the Aubrey circle provides the basis of an astronomical analysis later in the book, as does its metrological significance, which can only become recognised once there is an accurate survey plan of the monument.

An Original Bluestone Construction

Sometime after the Aubrey holes had been dug a compound semicircle made from pairs of bluestones was erected in the centre of the henge (*see overleaf*). Perhaps never finished, some of these bluestones were highly polished, tongue and grooved while others had holes to fit tenons in order to form the familiar trilithon so characteristic of the later sarsen stone constructions at Stonehenge.

This first stone (semi) circle was indeed a proto-Stonehenge, made from bluestones, and it was either not fit for purpose or fell out of fashion, for it was removed from the centre of the henge and 'stored' in order to make room for the larger and more imposing sarsen stones with its inner trilithon horseshoe. Only then were the bluestones reused, the less polished examples becoming the present bluestone circle, about 78 feet (23.8 m) in diameter and once comprising between 58 and 60 stones, now partly ruinous and placed concentrically between the sarsen circle and the sarsen trilithons. The slender shaped bluestones, which were the most polished stones on the site, became arranged in a horseshoe shape just within the trilithon horseshoe. There were originally 19 of these stones, some have their tenons visible, others have them smashed off, while two are grooved on one side. The best example of a sculpted and polished bluestone (stone 36 on the plan) was exhumed in the 1950s from beneath the bluestone circle, hosed off, photographed and then immediately returned to its hole, taking conservation to a new level in overcautiousness. The finest stone on the entire site, nobody now gets to see it!

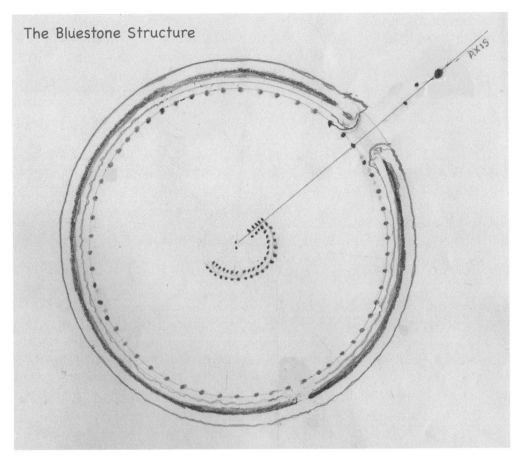

The bluestone double stone semi-circle, around 2700 BC. These were the first stones to be employed within the circular henge, and are thought to have been part of a project that was abandoned once the feasibility of moving the really huge sarsen stones became possible, after 2700 BC. The remains of this structure then were reused to form the present bluestone circle and the nineteen stone bluestone ellipse or horseshoe.

The First Geometrical Stone Construction at the Henge

A century or two after the Aubrey circle had been constructed, four sarsen stones were arranged as an accurate rectangle, each corner defined by placing a stone on its circumference. One of the holes dug to house one of these corner 'stations' (Stone 94) cut right across an Aubrey hole, but the others were not dug into existing Aubrey holes nor do they align to the spacing between the Aubrey holes. This strongly supports that the four Station stones are a later construction than the Aubrey circle holes. These stones or their holes are numbered 91 to 94 on the official plan, although two of the stones, 92 and 94, have long vanished from the site.

These stones represent the first sarsen stone geometry on the Stonehenge site, and this plus their arrangement as the four corners of a rectangle placed very close to the circumference of the Aubrey circle provides the entry point for the exploration of Stonehenge's astronomy, geometry and metrology, as we will discover in the next chapter.

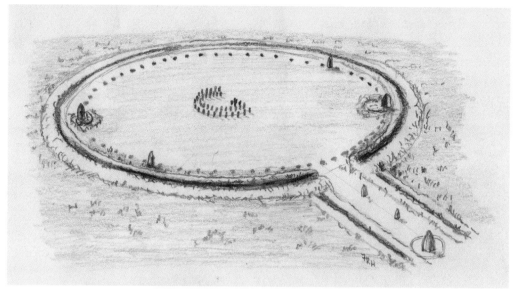

The Station Stone rectangle was defined by four large sarsen stones arranged on or very near to the perimeter of the Aubrey hole circle, around 2700 BC. The stones are numbered, from bottom left, clockwise, from 91 to 94. Stones 91 and 93 remain on site, the other two have long disappeared. The bluestone semi-circle, although shown above, may well have disappeared before the four Station stones were erected.

The Sarsen Circle and the Five Trilithons

The sarsen circle together with the trilithon horseshoe form the largest stone structures on the site. They form the part of the monument that is the most striking, through their size and particularly their height. Visually they are quite unlike any other original stone circle in Britain. The sarsens were dragged from the Marlborough Downs to be shaped, pounded, pummelled and polished off with thousands of sarsen mauls in order to form the sarsen circle, once comprising thirty upright stones and thirty lintels held aloft the uprights by jointing them in two planes, a level ring held above the ground at a height of over four metres (13 feet). Inside this closed structure, an even larger construction of five separate trilithons was erected on an elliptical perimeter, known as the trilithon horseshoe. Two of these massive structures had fallen, one as recently as 1800, but was carefully re-erected in 1958 such that the visitor can today glean some sense of the horseshoe shape of the whole assembly of inner trilithons. Unlike the sarsen circle they are graded in height from north to south, and the tallest stones on the entire site were the two middle uprights, stone 55 and 56 on the old Petrie numbering scheme and plan. Stone 55 has been uprooted and lies into two pieces across the Altar stone, adjacent to the lintel that once rose twenty-two feet above the ground. To prove this claim, Stone 56 sports a mighty conical tenon on its flat top.

This brief order of works is intended only as a first stop for those unfamiliar with the chronology of the monument whose many stages and phases became we now call Stonehenge. There are a wide range of first class books that cover these constructional stages in much more detail, for the more determined reader. The more recent of these are not necessarily better than some of the older books, one of the best of which we will meet in the next section.

Two of the massive trilithons are shown to the right of this photograph. Once five of these structures stood, their heights rising towards the axis of the monument. Stone 56, the highest stone still standing at Stonehenge, 22 feet off the ground, can been seen on the left, with a conical tenon joint on its top surface. Its companion, stone 55, has fallen, and lies in two bits over the altar stone, while the huge lintel lies adjacent (*see also page vi, and use the illustrations on page xii and 18 to assist in navigating around the monument*).

Chapter Three

The Importance of a Decent Site Plan

The leading expert on the archaeology of Stonehenge during the second half of the last century was Professor Richard Atkinson (Cardiff). Atkinson excavated much of the site during the early 1950s and one outcome was his book *Stonehenge* (Hamish & Hamilton, 1956). This became that rarest of books, both a popular success and a classic archaeological textbook. The book can still be highly recommended, for although the chronology has since been pushed back by nearly a thousand years, following the later introduction of radiocarbon dating techniques, each feature of the monument remains in its correct relative order of construction.

Atkinsons's authoritative manner and elegant demeanour was such that he had become the media's spokesperson in popularising prehistoric archaeology. The bow tie and cigarette holder no doubt helped in that regard, but in addition to these suave *accoutrements*, the man had a remarkable presence, and he did look a fair bit like Richard Burton. In 1970, while working on the BBC *Chronicle* documentary, *Cracking the Stone Age Code*, Atkinson and Thom had become unlikely friends, and in 1971 Atkinson approached Alexander Thom, and asked him if he would undertake an accurate survey of Stonehenge. Thom had previously pointed out to him that the then Ministry of Works plan of Stonehenge, a plan found in almost every brochure and book on the monument, was 'laughably bad', and had been astonished at its appalling inaccuracies.

In 1993, I asked Dr Archibald Thom, Alex Thom's son, some questions about this survey in a personal letter, to which he wrote back,

'About our survey, the Ministry plan was a botch. It had two scales on itself which did not fit. It had obviously been made up from several sources.

This finally persuaded A.T. (Alexander Thom) to do the survey. He never trusted the work of strangers. We carefully left records of where our survey pegs had been; nobody ever asked us about it all. Our survey is the best record of things on the surface. I still keep the tracings for reproduction. We measured the stone positions to half an inch, and then repeated the measurement at original ground level, about three feet up, according to what Dick (Richard Atkinson) told us."

Of all other plans it is not easy to be kind. The Ministry of Works (MoW) plan still remains the plan used by nearly all researchers who work with the physical layout of Stonehenge, and it is seriously flawed, surely the most glaring confirmation of the consequences of academic failure to recognise the importance of an accurate plan. Petrie must be rotating in his grave.

This long awaited survey of Stonehenge was eventually undertaken in 1973, by Professor Thom, then 79 years of age, by request from Professor Richard Atkinson following an earlier request to the custodians of the monument with his personal recommendation. It is beyond belief that no decent plan was readily available prior to 1973. The grant to finance this long overdue surveying project came not from Britain but from a most unlikely source, Case Western University in Cleveland, Ohio, courtesy of Robert Merritt and the Lloyd Foundation.

Richard Atkinson

Alexander Thom's 1973 Survey Plan of Stonehenge

Thom's survey plan was based on a seven station closed traverse, a self-checking surveying method. The plan is acknowledged to be the most accurate plan ever drawn up of the monument at ground level and it even gives the site's contours. Undertaken by Thom and his son Dr Archibald Thom with Richard Atkinson, the survey was also assisted by archaeologist Major Lance Vatcher, pioneer archaeoastronomer 'Peter' Newham and several members of the Survey Branch of the Royal School of Artillery surveying team. A copy of the 1:250 survey plan is illustrated opposite, taken directly from the master drawing (1:84) and given to the author by the late Archibald Thom.

Once an accurate plan became available, it also became possible to revisit the various stages of construction and ask sharper questions about the monument. Most specifically, the astronomy, geometry and metrology

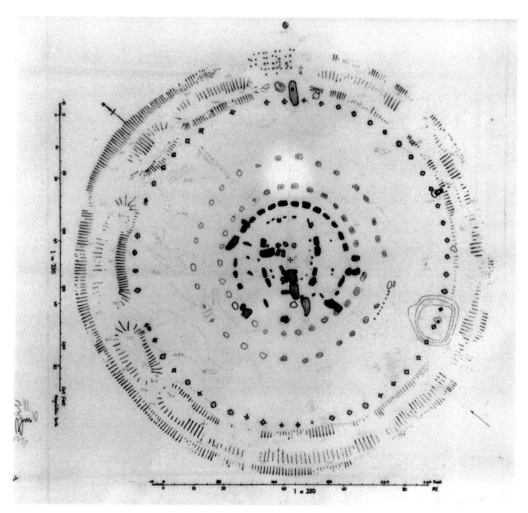

The 1973 survey plan of Stonehenge, undertaken by Alexander Thom, Lance Vatcher, Richard Atkinson and assisted by some Royal Artillery surveyors. This is the author's copy, taken from the original master plan, with the standing stones blacked in, the fallen stones shaded and missing stones or their holes left as outlines.

of the monument can be attempted with much more confidence. That confidence can only arise if the reader has access to either a copy of the plan or can read about how the survey was undertaken. The original source documents from the survey and analysis undertaken by Thom was only ever published in the academic *Journal for the History of Astronomy*.

The Early Days of Stonehenge, 3150 – 2700 BC

Following the construction of the ditch and bank, which has been dated at around 3150 BC, the first stage in the eventual building of the composite monument we now call Stonehenge was to dig 56 holes, the Aubrey circle, spaced to form a circle whose centre lies within a few centimetres of the geometrical centre of the henge. The 56 holes were each nominally circular, although very varied in diameter, from 0.75 to 1.7m. They originally had vertical sides and were flat bottomed, with depths varying from 0.61m to 1.14 m. This all seemed very imprecise until the radius of the whole circle had been surveyed and measured. Following the Thom survey in 1973, the Aubrey ring could then be confidently described by Thom as 'a circle with each hole accurately radially placed on a radius of 141.8 ft'. The circumferential spacing was found to be less accurate.

Thom's 1974 article in the *Journal for the History of Astronomy* revealed how this was done,

'In 1973 Lance Vatcher and Richard Atkinson by laborious prodding located accurately the outlines of all the Aubrey holes which were accessible. The centres of the shapes so marked out on the ground were indicated by metal stakes or by holes drilled in the disks of concrete previously placed to mark some of the holes, and these stakes and drilled holes were surveyed accurately by us.

The statistical centre and radius of the Aubrey ring was then found by the method described in Megalithic Sites in Britain. The standard deviation of the radii to the holes is 0.56 ft and the mean radius is 141.80 ± 0.08 ft'.

JHA, Vol 5 Part 2, No 13 June 1974, pp 81-90.

Thom's survey of Stonehenge included a ten-day workout with archaeologists Richard Atkinson and Lance Vatcher identifying the centres of all the (known) holes of the Aubrey circle where once there had been placed…well, in 1973 there was no archaeologically acceptable answer as to what these 56 holes had once held. Apparently they had no purpose at all, they were merely 56 holes dug inside the outer bank and ditch. Having dug these apparently pointless holes, it appears they were back-filled almost immediately afterwards, perhaps around 2700 BC and later some of these holes had had cremated remains placed into them.

Obtaining the best estimate possible for the diameter of the Aubrey circle was crucial to understanding the subsequent geometrical design and the metrology of the monument. The 1973 survey plan provided the answer just as popular interest in Stonehenge was reaching a new peak.

In the 1960s, three astronomers, 'Peter' Newham, Dr Gerald Hawkins and perhaps the most famous cosmologist of that time, Professor Sir Fred Hoyle, had all made significant contributions in identifying a unique astronomical purpose met by having 56 markers placed in a circle. Only this number of markers placed around the circumference of a circle can provide an accurate analogue of the motions of sun and moon around the stars, and also predict eclipses. This outstanding contribution to understanding the earliest phase of Stonehenge was hardly noticed by mainstream archaeology, and in truth hardly mattered to a world that was then preparing to put a man on the moon. To an astronomer, what had once briefly been placed into the holes was rendered unimportant in comparison to their number (56) and overall shape (circular), which provided an astronomical purpose for the Aubrey holes (*see below*).

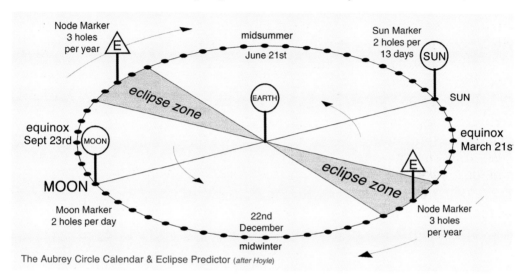

The Aubrey Circle Calendar & Eclipse Predictor (*after Hoyle*)

The Aubrey soli-lunar calendar (*after Hoyle*). In the mid-60s, cosmologist Professor Sir Fred Hoyle discovered that the 56 markers holes/posts/stones arranged around a circle could provide the simplest analogue model of the motions of the sun and moon, and also predict when eclipses were likely. Here is a stylised illustration showing a full moon on April 12th, with no chance of an eclipse. At Stonehenge, the six foot (2m) high walls of the original bank could have represented the circle of the ecliptic and Zodiacal stars.

In the mid 1990s, the author of an epic book *Stonehenge, Neolithic Man and the Cosmos* (Harpers, 1996), archaeologist John North broke rank and suggested that the 'later' cremations found in some of the Aubrey holes were a 'red herring'. Suddenly what had previously been carved on archaeological tablets of stone was being seriously questioned. North even included the use of Thom's 'archaeologically forbidden' megalithic yard in his analysis of the monument. It gradually became possible in academic journals to also suggest that an early wooden 'henge structure' had once been placed in these holes (*after North*). In recent years this revision of thinking has taken another leap forward such that it is now being mooted that these 56 holes may once have held the larger portion of the infamous bluestones after they were gathered up from their short-lived time at the centre of the henge and prior to being reused in later developments at the site (*see appendix two page 98*).

Whether the Aubrey holes may originally have held a circle of bluestones, and how the bluestones arrived at Stonehenge remain two very contentious issues. Recent work by Professor Mike Parker Pearson and archaeologists at Aberystwyth and UCL, employing petrological and other analyses, claim that some of the larger examples originated from several specific outcrops on or near the main Preseli ridge of West Wales.

The Station Stones

Following the construction of the Aubrey circle four quite large sarsen stones were located very close to its perimeter. These stones defined the corners of an accurate rectangle, now referred to as the Station stone rectangle, and once described by Dr Aubrey Burl as 'a near-perfect rectangle'. The geometry theorem taught to schoolchildren, that

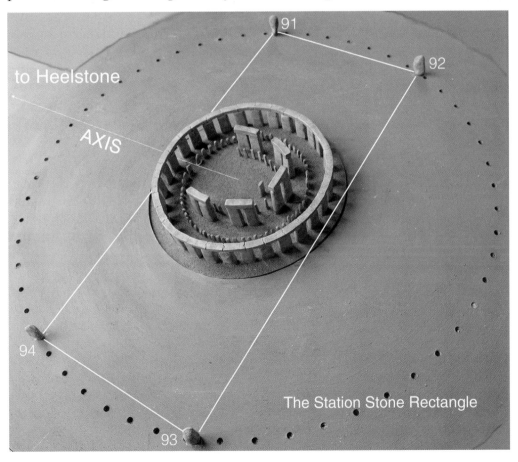

the angle contained within a semicircle (diameter) is always a right angle, proves the squareness of any apparently rectangular structure built with its corners on the perimeter of a circle. A further test, still used by all carpenters, bricklayers and surveyors is to compare the lengths of the diagonals of any rectangle to ascertain that they both measure the same length. The Station stone rectangle does this with an average accuracy of better than one part in 300, the rectangle is 'on the square' and all its angles can be confidently assumed to have been intended to be right angles. The abilities of the builders to accurately define right angles is seen measureably to be the case.

The Station stone rectangle is today without two of its corner stones, which have disappeared. Two of the original stones remain, a nine foot long irregular stone (stone 91) now recumbent and the other (stone 93) a four foot stump. The two missing stones (92 and 94) were once placed within roughly circular 'barrows' surrounded by a small ditch, and these features are shown on the plan. At the centre of the southern 'barrow' Colonel Hawley found a large stone hole that from its shape seemed likely to have once held the long vanished stone (Stone 92). The northern 'barrow' no longer has any visible sign of a central hole, although Atkinson noted that it may 'still be detected by probing'. [*Stonehenge, p 18*]. In 1978, this hole, once holding stone 94, was finally excavated. Cutting right through an already existing Aubrey hole, it confirmed that the Station stones were a later construction.

The Matter of Seven times Eight being Fifty-six

The Aubrey circle was just that, an accurate circle, whose circumference was marked out with 56 post-holes. Fifty-six is the product of seven and eight, therefore using the post-holes as a kind of megalithic 'cat's cradle' it is possible to construct the geometry of both the heptagon or octagon using long ropes, and if more complex geometrical complexity is required, these can become the heptagram and octagram (*see illustration over leaf*). Some recent writers on Stonehenge have assumed that the Station stone rectangle was intended to be based on octagonal geometry, yet any of the major plans or a review of the work of Petrie (1880), Thom (1973), or Atkinson (1978) will show that the Station stones (or their now long-vacant holes) are not aligned to the hole spacing 'quantum' of the fifty-six Aubrey holes. Indeed, none of the four are directly sited on an Aubrey hole, although one Station stone post-hole cuts through an Aubrey hole. Consequently the lengths of the shorter pair of sides measure slightly longer than would be expected from octagonal geometry.

A geometrical link within the various stages of Stonehenge. A seven-sided star constructed within a model of Stonehenge, by placing a peg in every eighth hole of the Aubrey circle, defines the circumference of the Sarsen circle. An inner heptagon then makes a good job determines the perimeter of the bluestone circle.

In 1976, Professor William Dibble of Brigham Young University, New York, submitted an article to the Journal for the History of Astronomy entitled '*A Possible Pythagorean Triangle at Stonehenge*' (*JHA* vol 7, 142-144). It came before Atkinson's study in the same journal entitled '*The Stonehenge Stations*'. (*JHA* vol 7, 145-148). Dibble suggested that the Station stones were placed in order to contain within their rectangular form the Pythagorean 5,12,13 triangle.

For those wishing to ponder further on the matter, here are some of the averaged measurements taken of the crossing angles of the two diagonals across the Station stone rectangle.

Flinder's Petrie (1880)
45.1°±0.1′ (least reliable from the data available and the assumptions that Petrie applied).

Alexander Thom (1973)
45.167° (average figure obtained by trigonometry by the author and taken from the original Thom survey)

Richard Atkinson (1978)
45.19° (from the *JHA* report)

These figures slightly favour the 5,12,13, at 45.24° rather than the octagonal geometry, at 45°. They do not tell us for sure whether or not a 5,12,13 triangle was intended, but neither do they confirm that the rectangle was based on the octagon. However, the verdict using geometry alone has to remain inconclusive (*see appendix three, page 100*).

John Michell later put this matter succinctly in a hand written letter he submitted with a diagram during the writing of *The Measure of Albion* (Bluestone Press, 2004), Both options are illustrated below, taken from Michell's original artwork and the accompanying hand written text.

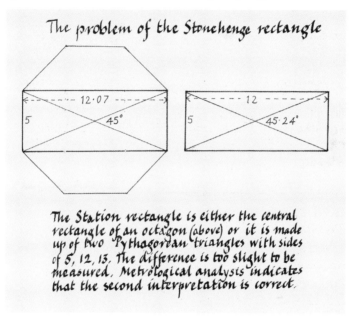

The *problem* of the Stonehenge rectangle

The Station rectangle is either the central rectangle of an octagon (above) or it is made up of two Pythagorean triangles with sides of 5, 12, 13. The difference is too slight to be measured. Metrological analysis indicates that the second interpretation is correct.

The Discovery of a Second 12:13 Ratio at Stonehenge

In the late 1970s, Alan Penny, who worked with Dr John Edwin Wood on some of the research presented in *Sun, Moon and Standing Stones* (OUP, 1980) noted that the distance from the Heel stone to the centre of the Aubrey circle is 'within a quarter of a metre of the length of the longer sides of the Station stone rectangle.' The Heel stone is thought to have been located prior to the Station stones, and the implication is that the builders were linking 'the new construction with the geometry of the existing monument'. This data is however no longer confined to geometry, it is also about lengths, about metrology, and another significant fact had emerged - the distance from the Aubrey circle centre to the Heel stone and the diameter of the Aubrey circle form the ratio 12:13 to each other, to a high order of accuracy (*better than 0.2%, see appendix seven, page 104*).

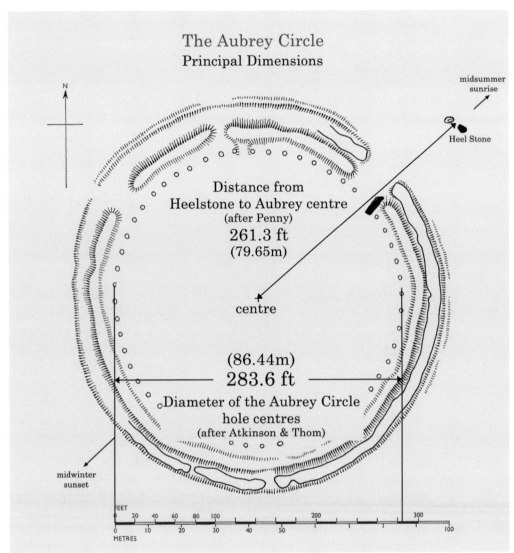

The Aubrey Circle
Principal Dimensions

N

midsummer
sunrise

Heel Stone

Distance from
Heelstone to Aubrey centre
(after Penny)
261.3 ft
(79.65m)

centre

(86.44m)
283.6 ft
Diameter of the Aubrey Circle
hole centres
(after Atkinson & Thom)

midwinter
sunset

FEET
0 20 40 60 80 100   200   300

0   10   20   30   40   50   100
METRES

The two principal dimensions built into the earliest phase of Stonehenge. They form an 12:13 ratio to each other, to 99.8% accuracy. A link with the 5,12,13 triangle?

Here emerges a second example of twelve and thirteen expressed as a ratio and found contemporaneous with the earliest features of Stonehenge, strongly supporting that the Station stone rectangle was based on 5,12,13 geometry. It certainly suggests that the builders of Stonehenge were working with the 12:13 ratio, and that it was important to them, because it was incorporated within very significant parts of their monument, the original axis of the monument (12 units), within the diameter of the

Aubrey circle (13 units), as the longer side of the Station stone rectangle (12), plus the already mentioned diagonal as the hypotenuse of a 5,12,13 triangle, *aka* the Aubrey diameter(also 13 units).

Using geometry alone, this matter is showing a level of precision that the model of prehistory cannot reckon with. There is a let-out clause, however, for owing to the large size of the stones chosen to mark the corners of the Station stone rectangle there will always be a problem knowing where precisely its corners were originally intended to be located. Atkinson (*op cit, p.18*) picked up on this important point,

> '*One need not suppose, of course, that the existing Station stones, or their vanished fellows, were actually used as surveyor's reference-points, for which they are far too large and imprecise; but rather that they form permanent and symbolic memorials of an operation of field geometry which, if it were to be repeated today, would tax the skill of many a professional surveyor.*'

So the 'scattered groups of savages' who became barbarians, so described in Atkinson's *Stonehenge* (p. 143) as secondary neolithic cultures, appear to have possessed considerable talent in precision field surveying. They built the Aubrey circle and the Station stone rectangle long before the major works of the later sarsen monument, the sarsen circle and the trilithon horseshoe. Of this later period of construction, Atkinson muses,

> '...*were these Wessex chieftains alone responsible for the design and construction of this last and greatest monument at Stonehenge? For all their evident power and wealth, and for all their widespread commercial contacts, these men were essentially barbarians. As such, can they have encompassed unaided a monument which uniquely transcends all other comparable prehistoric building in Britain, and indeed in all Europe north of the Alps, and exhibits so many refinements of conception and technique? I for one do not believe it*'(*page 163*).

These two quotes are very revealing. In the first quote Atkinson concedes that the 'savages' were better surveyors than the later barbarians, these same savages having shown to have known some quite advanced geometry and could construct circles, squares, triangles and rectangles to a high level of precision, at a level that 'would tax the skill of many a professional surveyor.' There comes a point where it is interesting to ponder the implications of the fact that Stonehenge could only begin to become recognised as a precision instrument once precision instruments had been developed to measure it and from which an accurate plan could be drawn up. So, just who were the barbarians until that point was reached?

Despite the mounting evidence, in the second quote Atkinson cannot bring himself to believe that the later barbarians could have 'encompassed unaided' the later constructions at the site. In these emotive and uncharacteristic outbursts one can picture 'Dickie' Atkinson chewing ever harder on his cigarette holder, as he confronted the schism between his findings at Stonehenge and the 1950s model of prehistoric Britain. Sadly, he lacked the resources then to begin the comprehension of megalithic science. To archaeologists of this period it seemed impossible that knowledge of Pythagorean triangles existed in Neolithic Britain, or that accurate surveying skills had been applied at the larger sites, yet here was evidence to support both suppositions.

All of this doubt and disbelief was typical of the time, but Atkinson later experienced a 'road to Damascus' moment, after which he embraced many of Thom's conclusions concerning the capabilities of the megalith builders. But what is more interesting about this retro-analysis of the period is that there was already, in the 1950s, enough information available such that a sixth-form maths student could have analysed the evidence and made progress at understanding the science that underpinned it.

If geometry alone could not decide the matter of the Station stones' geometry, then simple measurements taken from off the plan by Alan Penny provided a second 12:13 ratio, which supported the idea that knowledge of 5,12,13 geometry as employed in the later Station stone rectangle was already extant. Evidently, the ratio 12:13 was a big deal, so much so that it was incorporated at least twice into the monument's design.

The Accuracy and Dimensions of the Aubrey Circle

Thom's radial spacing for the Aubrey circle gives a figure for the diameter of the Aubrey circle centres to be 283.6 ft. These remain the best measurements available. If the Station stone rectangle is assumed to have been laid out on the perimeter of the Aubrey circle then this is also the length of each of the two diagonals of the rectangle, the length of the 'missing' thirteen sides required to complete four 5,12,13 triangles, from the constructed corners of the 5:12 rectangle. Using this diameter and by applying Pythagoras' theorem, the length of the '12' side and that of the '5' side can then be calculated as 261.78 ft, and 109.07 ft respectively. Expressed in units of Thom's megalithic yard of 2.722 ft, these dimensions present as follows,

'5' side = 109.07 ft	(40.07 MY)
'12' side = 261.78 ft	(96.17 MY)
'13' side = 283.6 ft	(104.19 MY)

Why use feet, in a metric age? The stock answer is that the metre was a Napoleonic rather than Neolithic unit of length, a relative newcomer to the metrological stables. There are other reasons. Thom's survey plan was produced with horizontal and vertical scales *in feet*. So was nearly every other plan. And the system of ancient metrology is based on the foot.

Books on Stonehenge often convert dimensions into metres and either fail to use the correct conversion figures, or round figures up or down to the nearest decimetre, which can hardly assist in any assessment of precision of the stone's locations or its role in any consequent geometry. However, for those who want their Stonehenge in metres the conversion factor is 3.2818399 feet = one metre; or one foot = 0.3047071m. For accurate work it is far better to read dimensions directly from a decent plan, in any units one chooses.

The near-integer value of each of the sides of the triangle expressed in megalithic yards suggests a strong metrological intention that the aim was to create a 5:12 rectangle in units of 8 MY, but there is still more that can be done to support this suggestion.

Finding the Unit Length

The measurements offer a more detailed way of discovering the unit of length intended by the designer(s) of the rectangle. If the perimeter length of the above 5,12,13 triangle is determined, by summing the individual side lengths, then a division by 30 (= 5 + 12 + 13) will reveal the best estimate of the unit of length employed in the construction.

So, add the three lengths, 104.19MY + 96.17MY + 40.07MY = 240.42 MY, and the best estimate of the unit of length is therefore,

$$240.42 \text{ MY} / 30 = \textbf{8.01433 MY}$$

A value of 8 MY for the intended unit length is a valid assumption, better than to 1 part in 500. Given the size of the rectangle and the limitations of using ropes or rods, this represents a unexpectedly accurate, even impressive, achievement. They are the kind of figures one might expect from a field surveying exercise undertaken without modern surveying instruments and led by an experienced surveyor backed by a coordinated group of 'chainmen'. This level of precision, found at Stonehenge, would, in Atkinson's own words, 'tax the skill of a modern field surveyor'.

Using first the geometry of the plan, and then applying simple metrological methods, the most likely unit of length has been revealed. That unit of length turns out to be eight of Thom's megalithic yards, within one part in five hundred. Well fancy that!

The Astronomy of the Station Stone Rectangle

Exploring the astronomical properties of the rectangle can begin with a little bit of history, made by Mr Cecil August Newham, an unsung hero of Stonehenge research during the 1960s. Here is a quote from Alexander Thom on the astronomy of the Station stone rectangle,

> *'Early in 1963, C A Newham drew attention to the fact that the long sides of the station rectangle indicated the moon setting in its extreme north position. It is reasonable to conclude that Stonehenge was a lunar as well as a solar observatory but no accuracy could have been been possible if the backsites and foresights were confined to the monument itself.'*

Newham, preferred to be known as Peter for reasons one might be able to guess. He was a serious researcher who undertook archaeo-astronomical surveys with a theodolite at Stonehenge during the last period when it still remained possible to walk in and more or less make any observation and measurement one fancied. Newham single-handedly made huge strides in understanding the relationship between the astronomical thinking behind the geometric construction of Stonehenge, so much so that his work was later incorporated by Gerald Hawkins within his bestselling book, *Stonehenge Decoded*, in 1965. Newham's contribution is acknowledged widely throughout the book, even his first entry into the public domain, an article in the Yorkshire Post on March 16th 1963, is mentioned. This article, Newham's finest hour, preceded by six months Hawkins' first paper on Stonehenge astronomy, published in *Nature*.

In 1963 the car-park post holes had recently been discovered, and Newham surveyed them from the henge. He published a booklet, *The Astronomical Significance of Stonehenge*, which sold well at the monument. During his survey at Stonehenge in the 1970s Thom took up this new discovery, and found,

> *'The azimuth of the line joining the South Station near the Aubrey ring to the stone at the northwest corner is about 320 degrees, and the line to Gibbet Knoll (azimuth 320° 02') passes between the centre and east (car-park) holes. We shall give a reason for these peculiar posts. The car park is below the level of Stonehenge and so a high structure would be needed to cut the horizon. This explains why such massive posts were used.'* (JHA, op cit)

There was a not insignificant chronological problem of the five thousand year dating difference between the Station stones and the car-park post holes. Wooden posts do not normally last this long. Recognising this fact, Thom undertook a survey to look beyond the post holes that mark the major standstill setting point of the moon. Nine miles distant and just above Market Lavington he found a putative horizon marker for the most northerly moonset, at Gibbet Knoll. The alignment passed directly over the car-park post holes when viewed along the southern side of the Station stone rectangle.

The Geometry of the Sun and Moon at Stonehenge

In the 1973 *Journal for the History of Astrononomy* report on his work at Stonehenge, Thom did not draw enough attention to an important fact concerning the latitude of Stonehenge. At the latitude of Stonehenge, 51° 10′ 42″ the horizon positions of the major standstill moon and the solstitial sun, both rises and sets, form an accurate right angle to each other. In the *JHA* article Thom does gives the information, but in separate sections of the text. On the azimuth of the rise of the midsummer sunrise he gave 49° 57′ (with the sun half-risen along the axis) and for the set of the most northerly major standstill moonset horizon point he gave 320° 02′ to Gibbet Knoll). These two azimuth angles enclose an angle of 89° 55′, effectively a right angle. Similarly, the most southerly moonrise during a major standstill forms a right angle to the midwinter sunset point.

What was astonishing was that Thom failed to capitalise on the link between the latitude, the astronomy and the geometry. The four sides of the Station stone rectangle are aligned to these specific four directions, the longer sides to the lunar standstill angles, one moonrise and one moonset angle, and the shorter sides to the solstice angles, again one sunrise and one sunset angle. The rectangle thus represents a soli-lunar structure that can only be constructed near the latitude of Stonehenge, or it will not align. Too north or south of Stonehenge, or if the horizon angles are raised too much when viewed from another location, and the whole structure morphs into a parallelogram, whose four corners can no longer can be placed around the perimeter of a circle.

Hawkins (*op cit*) had made much of this feature in his original paper in *Nature*, whose specialist readers evidently also failed to see the significance in this collection of facts about Stonehenge. In *Stonehenge Decoded* he later discussed the implications in detail,

> '*The angles between the extreme sun and moon positions are awkward angles. Furthermore they are set by the Creator, and not rearrangeable by man. It would be next to impossible to align stones geometrically on the ground and celestially to all those positions and yet keep the distances between those stones in round numbers of a single unit of distance.*' ......'*In other words, in the northern hemisphere there is only one latitude for which, at their extreme declinations, the sun and*

moon azimuths are separated by 90 degrees. Stonehenge is within a few miles of this latitude. …. It seems unlikely that the choice of 51.178 degrees as a location for Stonehenge was made by chance.'

The choice of Stonehenge's location had already been made before the building of the rectangular design of the Station stone rectangle. It would be a bizarre coincidence indeed were they to have chosen this location and then discovered that it just happened to fit the rectangular nature of extreme sun and moon rise and set events. It would be far more likely that the site was found by trial and error over many years, and that the builders already knew of the astronomical uniqueness of the latitude. If so, the architects of Stonehenge would have had some appreciation of the effects on observations of the celestial bodies as one travelled north or south, i.e. they understood the effects of latitude. The story being told in this book will suggest that they may even have been able to measure latitude.

The information concerning the Stonehenge site during its early period has now built up to a point where it can provide many significant leads concerning a functional purpose for the astronomy, geometry and metrology of the monument. An answer to the question: Why Stonehenge? is beginning to emerge.

1. The site appears to have been used in mesolithic times for the erection of three large posts arrayed to the northwest of the present Stonehenge. From somewhere at that location, several thousand years prior to the building of the ditch and bank, the posts would show the most northerly major standstill moonset position.

2. Following the construction of the ditch and bank, from the centre of the resulting henge, the axis of the early monument was aligned to the solstitial sunrise and sunset positions through the gap in stones arranged in pairs to form portals. Today these stones are represented only by the Heel stone and its adjacent post hole, the Slaughter stone, and its adjacent post hole, and the massive trilithon stones 55 and 56, one of which has fallen and broken into two parts over the Altar stone.

3. The Aubrey circle was constructed from the centre of the henge. Fifty-six large holes were dug to a radius of 141.8 ft ± 0.08 ft (Thom survey). The diameter, hole centre to opposite hole centre, was therefore 283.6 ft (86.44m). Posts or bluestones may have originally been placed in these holes. The average spacing between these holes was 15.91 ft.

4. According to the top British cosmologist of the time, Professor Fred Hoyle, 56 holes around a circle represents the lowest number

that both enables the positions of the sun and moon to be accurately tracked, and eclipse times to be predicted.

5. The distance from the Heel stone to the centre of the Aubrey circle compared to the diameter of the Aubrey circle form the ratio 12:13 to 99.8% accuracy.

6. The four Station stones were later arranged on or very near the perimeter of the Aubrey circle to define the corners of an accurate rectangle, whose longer sides measure just under 262 ft (79.8m). This is the same distance as that between the Heel stone and the Aubrey centre, and therefore, with the Aubrey diameter, forms two sides of a Pythagorean 5,12,15 triangle within the Station stone rectangle, the entire construction fabricated using a unit of 8 megalithic yards of 2.722 ft (0.8297m).

7. The orientation of the Station stone rectangle was aligned to both the positions of the maximum major standstill moonrise and set, and the midsummer sunrise - midwinter sunset axis. The extreme rises and sets of the sun and the moon can be observed along the sides of the Station stone rectangle. This feature can only be successfully achieved within a few miles of the latitude of Stonehenge or by adjusting the horizon altitude from the observing position. This latter option was selected at Bryn Celli Ddu, on Anglesey. Here the topology of the natural horizon is elevated around the point where the midsummer sun rises. Its azimuth in 3000 BC was 53.15°, and that of the extreme moon set was 323.20°, the included angle is almost a right angle. (for more information and full survey data on Bryn Celli Ddu visit the skyandlandscape website).

The Station Stone Rectangle: Conclusions

The builders could have placed the corners of any proportion of rectangle, even a square, around the Aubrey circle, but they chose a ratio of 5:12 in units of 8MY, which automatically gave diagonal lengths of 13 in the same units. The ratio 12:13, to a high accuracy, and in the same units, had already been built into the axis, between the Heel stone to Aubrey centre, and the diameter of the Aubrey circle (*see illustration, page 36*). This suggests prior knowledge of the 5,12,13 triangle because the units of length of the 12:13 ratio are the 8 MY previously chosen for the design of the Heel stone axis arrangement. It therefore follows that the Aubrey circle diameter was deliberately chosen to be 13 units of 8 MY and the Heel stone then placed to form the 12:13 ratio to this diameter. Why was 12:13 so significant, and what is so special about a 12:13 ratio, or a 5,12,13 triangle, or even 8 megalithic yards? Time to meet the lunation triangle.

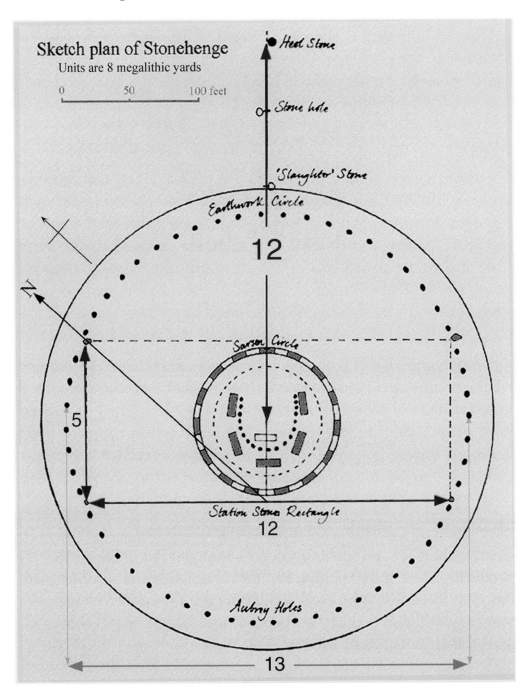

Sketch plan of Stonehenge
Units are 8 megalithic yards

0   50   100 feet

Heel Stone

Stone hole

'Slaughter' Stone

Earthwork Circle

12

Sarsen Circle

5

Station Stones Rectangle
12

Aubrey Holes

13

In this chapter the simple number ratios built into the earlier phases of Stonehenge, 12:13 and 5:12, in units of 8 megalithic yards, will be seen to provide a toolbox with which to integrate the astronomy, geometry and metrological qualities of the monument.

PART TWO

Chapter Four

The Lunation Triangle
Cosmology on a Rope

In this chapter a major new component is revealed, one which synthesizes the existing data from the last chapter to enlarge megalithic capability. Previously, an accurate circular model of the motions of the sun and moon was found to have been the first construction to be placed within the newly made henge. This device enabled the seasons, the date within the year, the lunar position against the stars and its phase to be known, or predicted in advance. It could also directly record or predict the dates of full and new moons, and it could inform the operator when an eclipse was possible. Taken separately from the other features within Stonehenge it is unlikely that one could prove the Aubrey circle of 56 markers was ever used this way.

However, within the bank and ditch, simple ratios had also been incorporated within the earlier stages of Stonehenge. These manifested as lengths between key parts of the monument and when a common unit of length - eight megalithic yards - was applied, all these lengths became whole numbers of that unit, 5, 12 and 13. Furthermore, within the monument was built a rectangular structure that aligned to the extreme sun and moon positions, something which could only be attained at or very near the latitude of Stonehenge and which also contained a Pythagorean 5,12,13 triangle.

The orbital numbers of the earth and moon, expressed as days, are not convenient whole-number relationships, nor simple fractional arrangements. The numbers, as a linear or one-dimensional count, do not reveal any obvious or immediate pattern or rhythm. There are 365.2422 days in the cycle of the year and the phases of the moon take 29.53059 days to complete one cycle. However, the astronomical reality of the cosmic dance being enacted around our planet is that even the most basic of observations, a day count or tally, will reveal that sometime after twelve lunar months (the lunar year) have been observed, and before thirteen lunar months have elapsed, one seasonal or solar year of 365 days has taken place. The lunar month averages just over 29.53 days in length and this time period is also known as the *synodic month* or *the lunation period*.

What is revealed by sun and moon watching is an emerging relationship between 12 and 13, only when these numbers expressed as lengths of time - *in units of lunar months*. The length of time it takes one year to complete occurs after observing the twelfth and before observing the thirteenth lunar months or lunation. An observer of the skies could obtain this knowledge within a single year. What is actually observed in the sky is that after a solar tropical year has elapsed the moon is seen to have passed through twelve phase cycles and then advanced on by about a third of a cycle. If on the first of January the moon is observed as a thin crescent in the early evening skies, then a year later, on the same date, it will be gibbous, becoming a full moon within a week.

Surely, the natural next stage in any process of recording this interelationship between the sun and moon would be to want to find out exactly where the solar year would end between that twelfth and thirteenth lunar month.

It is assumed by almost all archaeologists and historians that numbers and arithmetic were beyond the minds of people in the Neolithic period. This assumed lack of numeracy does not prevent counting, nor extend into the appreciation of shape, movement and proportion, something an ex-hunter gatherer may have excelled at, even perhaps rather better than we might. By analysing notches scored into bones, paleontologist Alexander Marshack claimed that tally counting of the lunar cycle had been undertaken as far back as 10,000 BC.

Tallying days and lunar months naturally reveals the regular rhythm described above, however crudely it is done, and the tally stick, notches, marks or posts can become our familiar ruler once the time period used for the count becomes a regularly spaced series of lengths. Tallying thus transduces time periods into lengths, so that the lunar month will be about twenty-nine plus a half 'day-lengths', or an almost exact fifty-nine 'day-lengths' over two lunar months. There may have been no number-names as such available to the neolithic astronomer, but once these lengths emerged from the tally device, they could be transferred, added end on end and otherwise manipulated in order to see the geometric and/or time relationships between sun and moon, and perhaps even the larger visible planets, venus, mars, jupiter and saturn.

These four planetary bodies would periodically be observed doing something the sun and moon never do, periodically making a retrograde or direct station, where they would be seen to stop against the backdrop of the stars for a period of time, then move backwards awhile for a length of time, before stopping once more and gradually resuming their normal anticlockwise motion with respect to the stars.

All of these observations would produce associated lengths in whatever unit of length had originally been chosen to determine the separation between tallying marks, be these one day or one lunar month apart. A complete astronomical knowledge of the sun, moon and solar system could be built up using such a method, over time, and containing stored information about calendar events and eclipse times. No arithmetic is required, just recording elapsed days, or months as regular intervals.

The Relationship between the Sun and Moon

This book concerns itself only with the motions and time periods of the solar year and lunar month or lunation period. A modern astronomy book will announce that the lunation period divides the solar year up 12.368267 times, this being the average number of lunar months in one solar year. The fractional part, 0.368267 lunar months, just over a third of a lunation, corresponds in time terms to a length of 10.875 days. It can almost exactly be expressed by the fraction 7/19, which is 0.368421 as a decimal fraction.

A neolithic astronomer would 'see' or comprehend this number in a completely different way, as a length, representing eleven tally lengths of day-recording. Three of these would not quite fit within the length that corresponded to a lunar month, overshooting it by three day-tally lengths. Although this is not the way that the comprehension of numbers is taught today in our schools, it is an alternative way of appreciating quantity, proportion, ratio and fractions.

In early 1988, I became aware that a 5,12,13 triangle can provide a two dimensional template for a simple geometrical construction whereby a remarkably accurate soli-lunar calendar could be produced, that is, a calendar where the length (of time) of the lunar month (or lunation period) of 29.53059 days became *automatically calibrated* within the overarching framework of the solar 'tropical' year of 365.2422 days duration. I termed this device a *lunation triangle*. This device accurately places where, during the thirteenth lunar month, the solar year becomes complete.

A Stone Age Technology Revisited

There are other aspects about the 5,12,13 triangle, inherent qualities that few people appreciate today. Firstly, it has integer lengths in all three of its sides, like all Pythagorean triangles. There are no fractional lengths. It can therefore be constructed using a single common unit of length, any length one likes, by measuring that chosen length out along a rope and marking the divisions. For a 5,12,13 triangle one requires thirty equal divisions, each of the length of the chosen unit.

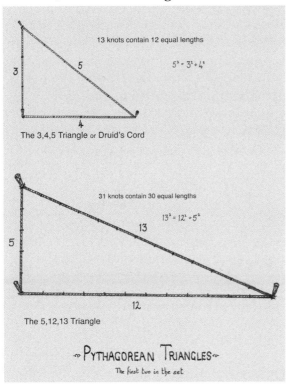

13 knots contain 12 equal lengths

$5^2 = 3^2 + 4^2$

5

3

4

The 3,4,5 Triangle or Druid's Cord

31 knots contain 30 equal lengths

$13^2 = 12^2 + 5^2$

13

5

12

The 5,12,13 Triangle

~ PYTHAGOREAN TRIANGLES ~
The first two in the set

A second advantage only becomes clear when this thirty division rope is being laid out on the ground - the right angle is *automatically* defined. Pegging the 'twelve' side down, the ends of the outlying 'five' and 'thirteen' side lengths are then brought together, and pegged into the ground. And there is the right angle, accurately constructed on the ground, no protractors necessary. Builders routinely use this technique to mark out the corners of their new buildings using a string, except they more commonly use the simpler 3,4,5 triangle, and sometimes even the 7,7,10 triangle if the corners are not required to be more accurate than to one degree.

Combining Geometry and Astronomy

Initially, I thought that the '12' and '13' sides of the triangle might represent, as a length, the time period for twelve and thirteen lunar months to have elapsed. This implied that the unit length of the triangle represented a (time) unit of one lunar month. The '12' side of the triangle thus represented twelve lunar months, which is 354.367 days, the lunar year, while the '13' side represented 13 lunar months, which is 383.89 days. It has to be possible to fit the length of the solar year, represented as 12.368.. lunar months, somewhere between these two time periods. The question was *where* and *how*?

The 5,12,13 triangle had now become a two dimensional geometric framework where the two longer sides represented 12 and 13 lunar months and framed a space within which the length of the solar year can be represented as a new line drawn between the apex of the triangle, its 'sharp end', and some point on the opposite '5' side of the triangle.

The trick is knowing where this constructed line must end, how to position it, and where its terminus is to be located on the '5' side. In other words, where to place the length of the solar year, as an additional 'intermediate hypotenuse', somewhere between the twelfth and the thirteenth synodic months, which will then automatically be divided up into 12.36826.. lunar months. Now for a Pythagorean surprise. The terminus point for this intermediate hypotenuse is located where the '5' side becomes divided into the ratio 3:2, musically the most harmonius interval, known as a 'fifth'. The 3:2 point is the terminus for the solar year line.

By combining astronomy within the geometry of the 5,12,13 triangle an unexpected connecting link between time and space is revealed. Whether or not this physical property is causal or acausal is not the purpose of this book (it is, however, certainly an interesting question to ponder). What needs to be thoroughly understood is that this simple Pythagorean triangle, modified into a lunation triangle, integrates the seemingly complicated motions of the sun and moon. In other words, it marries the sun and moon together, and it does this extremely well, entirely by using whole number ratios within the triangle, that represent lunar months. It produces only one fraction, the emerging 0.3682662 lunation fractional component, the 10.875 days, the 7/19ths tagged onto the end of the solar year rope, and which I have termed in earlier works *the silver fraction*.

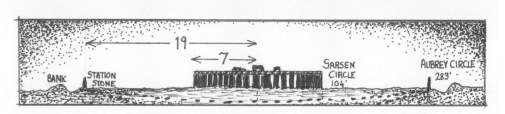

The *silver fraction* at Stonehenge. The diameters of the Aubrey and Sarsen circles form the ratio 7:19, and this is the secret of understanding the way the sun and moon interact in time. 7/19ths is 0.368 of a lunar month, and 12.368 lunar months make up the year.

Proto Stonehenge in Wales

THE CONSTRUCTION AND USE OF A LUNATION TRIANGLE

Mark a rope with thirty equal divisions along its length. Any length of division will suffice, provided the rope is long enough, but here I shall assume that the Megalithic yard (2.722 ft, 32.67 inches or 0.829 m) or a multiple will have been chosen, for reasons that are explained elsewhere in the text.

Once the rope has been marked up the procedure is as follows:

1. First peg what will become the '12' side by placing five divisions one side before the first peg and thirteen after the second. Twelve divisions are pegged out.

2. Swing the unpegged end of the '5' side and the unpegged end of the '13' side and bring these two ends together. Peg where the ends of the five and thirteen sides meet. Automatically this will both define the right angle and complete the 5, 12, 13 triangle. The two acute angles will also be accurately defined.

3. Rotate the end of the '13' side down towards the twelve side. When this side crosses over the end of the third division up from the '12' side, the 3:2 point of the '5' side, peg its end down, outside of the triangle. A new or intermediate hypotenuse has been created and the '3' side will now have 12.369 divisions within the triangle and 0.631 divisions outside.

4. The 0.369 of one division will be found to closely approximate to one foot, if the division marks have been spaced equally and defined accurately one megalithic yard apart.

5. The intermediate hypotenuse now represents the solar year already calibrated into lunar months. It may now be subdivided into 365.242 days, each division (one day) being 1.1035 inches (28.0) mm.

6. Full moon, new moons and quarter moons can all now be predicted in advance by successive halving of each division. This is best done by having a second rope marked up with the same unit length (1 MY) and folding it successively, once for the full and new moons and twice for the quarter moons.

7. Eclipse prediction. The 0.631 megalithic yard 'spare' end of the thirteen side rope, which has been languishing outside of the triangle, can now be folded back over the 3:2 point, and taken back along the intermediate hypotenuse – the solar year rope. The end of this folded back rope then marks the length of one eclipse year (346.6 days) from the apex of the triangle. Why this should be so is beyond the scope of this book, another astonishing gift delivered by the geometry of the lunation triangle.

8. Make up a second rope representing the eclipse year. Fold this 'eclipse year' rope in two and mark the fold to indicate the two 'eclipse seasons', one at the fold the other at the end. These eclipse seasons move backwards around the calendar by just under twenty days a year. This second rope can be slid along the 'year' rope and aligned to a previously observed eclipse, thereafter a full or new moon within fifteen days of the date coinciding with the position of either of the eclipse seasons will alert the astronomer that an eclipse may occur, although of course it may not be visible at that location. For a lunar eclipse to be visible the sun has to be below the horizon, for a solar eclipse to be visible the sun has to be above the horizon and the observatory has to be located on the narrow trackway of the shadow of the moon as it speeds across the earth's surface.

It is much easier to start building and using a lunation triangle than it is to describe this process in words. The device is a really effective way of keeping tabs on the calendar, and the sky, and for noting tide times and recording solar and lunar events. The intermediate hypotenuse, of 12.369 lunar months in the solar year is within 99.994% of the true figure, 12.368267 lunar months. This device is very accurate.

CONSTRUCTING A LUNATION TRIANGLE

The following diagrams formed the basis of practical instruction
given during many short courses and tutorials in the 1990s.
Constructing and using the lunation triangle on a flat field
was undertaken in order to then perform astronomical predictions
relating to full and new moon dates, moon phase and position
against the stars, eclipse prediction and times of high and low tides.

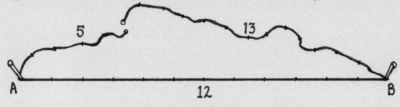

(i) Peg out '12' side of 5-12-13 triangle.

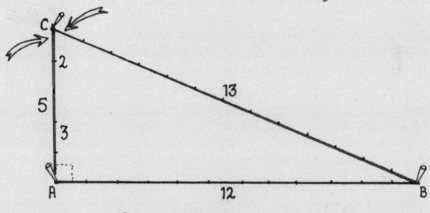

(ii) 'Close' triangle to define right angle.

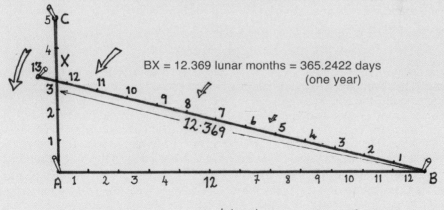

BX = 12.369 lunar months = 365.2422 days
(one year)

12.369

(iii) Bring '13' side down to '3:2' point on '5' side. Peg end.

51

The silver fraction is the secret of the whole sun-moon business, and it can be found at Stonehenge, where it is not hidden at all, it is found between the the the diameters of the two principal circles in the design of the monument, the Aubrey circle and the Sarsen circle. The outer diameter of the latter circle is given by North, Atkinson and others at 104.27 feet and the Thom survey surveyed the Aubrey circle to find its diameter to be 283.6 feet (86.44m). Divide one by the other and one gets 0.3674, which is 99.71% of 7/19ths. Stonehenge enshrines the secret of the sun and moon.

These kinds of numerical relationship do not fit within modern cosmology, being far too numinous for modern science to embrace, but one is still left with the strange fact that our observed experience of the main periods of the two luminaries, the complex dance of the sun and moon, can be arranged or choreographed within a simple two-dimensional geometry, a fact which no one, I am sure, can argue is other than remarkable.

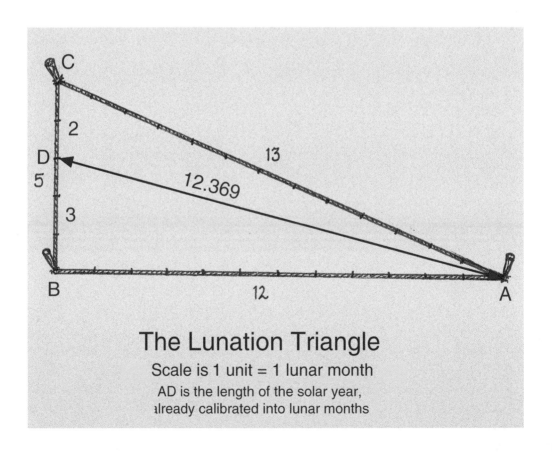

The Lunation Triangle
Scale is 1 unit = 1 lunar month
AD is the length of the solar year,
already calibrated into lunar months

Traditional Number Symbolism and the Lunation Triangle

Symbolically, within the traditional number sciences attributed to Vedic teachings, the Pythagoreans, Plato and the Druids, the lunation triangle places two pairs of numbers together that are each separately associated with masculine and feminine qualities. The lunation triangle presents them within a remarkably coherent synthesis, for the numbers 12 and 13 are associated with the solar and lunar qualities repectively, while in numerology 3 represents the first masculine number and 2 has always been the first feminine number. There is a new astronomical component, the lunation triangle 'marries' the sun and moon (*see appendix 8*).

Numerically and geometrically, once the 3:2 point has been found, the Pythagorean theorem enables a quick assessment of the length of the line, which I have called an *intermediate hypotenuse*, and it equals the square root of 153, (122 + 32). This is 12.369 lunations, and it represents the number of lunar months in one solar year to an astonishing accuracy. Using the 3:2 point creates a tiny error of just 31 minutes and 12 seconds in the length of the year, one part in 16,857. Most importantly to a practicing astronomer, the number of lunar months in the year are presented ready calibrated to the length of the solar year.

The question that naturally arises from the discovery of the lunation triangle is whether this type of triangular wizardry was a new discovery or might it have been known about in antiquity, a time when great efforts were made to marry the sun and the moon? If so, were there any surviving remains of these 'lunation' devices, and where might these be found? It has taken over twenty years to answer both these questions in the affirmative, and this quest is covered in a later chapter.

Combining Metrology within the Geometry and Astronomy

If the '12' and '13' sides of the triangle represent the time periods of twelve and thirteen lunar months respectively, then the physical unit of length chosen to construct the triangle becomes metrologically connected to this time period - the lunar month. For the Station stone rectangle the unit length was determined to be 8 megalithic yards (to within one part in 300). This unit must then represent the 8 lunation periods of 29.53059 days, in which case the intermediate hypotenuse length, 12.369 x 8 MY in length, becomes 98.95 MY. This is a highly significant result as it is the number of lunar months in 8 solar years.

Soli-Lunar Repeat Calendar Cycles

A day tally of lunar observations will record a period of time after twelve lunar months have elapsed and the end of one solar year. Following this period the moon will be 10.875 days into its thirteenth monthly cycle, having completed 12.368 lunations since the start of counting. This approximation to a third of a lunar advance each solar year will accrue year on year. After three solar years have elapsed, it will slightly exceed one complete additional lunation. There are other integer numbers of solar years where similar close soli-lunar 'repeats' are found. Surprisingly, there are four within the first twenty years (*see appendix six, page 54*).

Sun–Moon repeat calendar cycles

Elapsed Years	Lunations	Accuracy	Actual no. of Lunations	Elapsed Days	SITE EXAMPLE
3	37	+3.09 days	37.1047	1095.73	Le Manio, Carnac www.skyandlandscape.com
5	62	- 4.69 days	61.8413	1826.21	Coligny Calendar
8	99	- 1.59 days	98.9461	2921.94	Avebury Stonehenge (Station rectangle)
19	235	- 2.08 hours	234.9971	6939.60	Stonehenge (Bluestone horseshoe)

At various times and within various ancient civilisations, each of these repeat calendar cycles – 3, 5, 8 and 19 years - were employed. The Minoan culture adopted the 8 year cycle, the 'Early Jewish' calendar was also 8 years, prior to a later conversion to the 19 year Metonic cycle. The Romano-Celtic Coligny calendar appears to have employed the five year cycle. At megalithic sites, Avebury circle, with 98 or 99 huge stones in its perimeter, suggests a possible connection to the eight year cycle, while the nineteen polished bluestones in the innermost construction at

Stonehenge – the horseshoe ellipse – would suggest a connection with the nineteen year cycle. Of specific interest at Stonehenge is that had the Station stones been intended as the basis of a lunation triangle, *then the length of its intermediate hypotenuse, at 98.95 megalithic yards, would record the number of lunations in eight solar years.*

The clear choice of a multiple of eight times any given unit length chosen for the soli-lunar hypotenuse of a lunation triangle, suggests both acquired knowledge of the eight-year soli-lunar repeat cycle and that the built triangle was intended to be used to record a full 8 year cycle. At Stonehenge, because the unit length is 8 megalithic yards this represents eight lunation periods, in time terms. After eight years, there will have been just under 99 lunations.

The eight year repeat cycle must also include Venus in its whirling dance. Eight solar years is within just two days of the time taken for this planet to draw out a huge pentagon and its associate pentagram star around the Zodiac, easily observed through watching the behaviour of this planet against the fixed stars night on night during its periodic retrograde motion, every 584 days. Eight years from reading this paragraph, the sun, moon and venus will again be found very close to their present positions in the sky, against the fixed stars, because,

8 years of 365.2422 days	**= 2921.938 days**
99 lunar months of 29.53059 days	**= 2923.528 days**
5 Venus stations of 583.94 days	**= 2919.726 days**

Solving Storage Problems

Archaeoastronomers have long criticised the idea of megalithic precision astronomy because they have been unable to understand how, in a preliterate culture, such could have been possible without being able to store records of astronomical events. With knowledge of the lunation triangle this could easily be accomplished, and this may be why the geometrical basis of one can be found within the perimeter of the Aubrey circle at Stonehenge.

The lunation triangle is a mechanism that easily enables the storing of accurate astronomical data which is portable and can be 'replayed'. Ropes or rods can be placed end-on-end for longer time periods, or slid back and forth to investigate the inter-relationship between two time cycles. The lunation triangle makes it possible to fabricate, using rope or rods, a simple calendraic device for storing records concerning the timings of any past or present astronomical events. Future predictions can be made.

There are two ways to place the intermediate hypotenuse line correctly,

1. By previously ascertaining the length of the solar year, through direct astronomical observations. If a day count or a lunar month count for the whole year has been tallied the resulting length may be dropped into the 5,2,13 triangle, where the unit length has previously been chosen to be that of the lunar month tally, as indicated in the diagram. The tally line will then terminate on the 3:2 point.

2. By knowing the trick.

Once the constructional technique is known, then direct daily astronomical observations are no longer required. Having been shown the constructional procedure, and the geometrical trick of finding the 3:2 point, the lunation triangle then becomes a portable calendrical instrument which can be carried around or even worn around the body. What has happened or what is happening in the sky can now be read off this analogue model, easily constructed on the ground.

Whichever route is taken, the accuracy in defining the length of the solar year calibrated in lunar months is potentially 99.994%. The error is about a day after 46 years, or 1 part in 16,800.

The procedures above enable the geocentric motions of the sun and the moon as time periods to be subsequently stored as lengths. The lunation triangle therefore provides a precision recorder of key solar and lunar periods, and the observable events these bring about, in the form of new and full moons, tides and eclipses. Predictions can then be made concerning eclipses, tides and other relevant solar and lunar events.

The earlier Aubrey circle contained 56 markers around the perimeter of a circle. This number of markers happens to provide the simplest possible analogue device with which to represent the motions of the sun and moon on and around the ecliptic, and to provide warning of a potentially visible eclipse (Hoyle, *On Stonehenge* (1965) and Heath (*A Key to Stonehenge* et al, 1993, 1998). However, the Aubrey circle or a model of it is not readily portable nor does it inherently offer long-term storage of astronomical data.

Lunation Triangle – Historically True or False?

The lunation triangle is an abstracted calendar device. It allows an astronomer to work without looking up to the sky so often. It can bridge those times when visual records are unobtainable due to cloud. Once this little triangular trick has been demonstrated and understood, it is no longer necessary to make direct observations and estimates of the length of the year quite as often. Observations rendered impossible when it is rainy, cloudy or cold or on a very windy night (often all three when taking astronomical observations in Britain) may be avoided. It will still be necessary to confirm that the calendar remains synchronised to the seasons, to observe that on key dates the sun rises and sets where it always has done, that the moon is full or new on the date predicted, and whether or not that full or new moon is eclipsed on schedule. The astronomer will still need to observe solstitial sunrises or sets, and observe eclipses, those precise times when it is certain that the moon, full or new, is 'yoked together' (in *syzygy* or in line) with the earth and the sun.

Any 5,12,13 triangle found at a megalithic site, once its dimensions are accurately known, offers a researcher the opportunity to investigate whether it once formed the geometrical basis around which a lunation triangle could have been constructed. If this can be confirmed from the unit length and significant numerical ratios found existing between the unit length and astronomical time periods, the researcher no longer needs to be troubled over whether Neolithic communities knew the length of the solar year or the lunar year/month to high accuracies, but rather how these time periods (of the solar and lunar year) had been originally obtained. For it is impossible to create a lunation triangle without either having first established the length of the solar year and the lunar year by direct astronomical observations, or by being instructed in the inner construction, the geometrical 'trick' of the lunation triangle, which identifies the length of the solar year already calibrated into lunar months. However one gets to know that trick, someone, at some time previously, *must have worked the matter out from observational data*. The length of the solar year and that of the lunar month have to be known prior to discovering the lunation triangle.

If there was a lunation triangle ever associated with the Station stone rectangle at Stonehenge, the rectangle must have been built by people who understood the inner construction hidden within a 5,12,13 triangle, inherently part of the 5:12 rectangle. That would mean that prior to around 2750 BC, the observational techniques to establish the astronomical periods of the solar year and lunar month to high accuracy had already been mastered. To a conventional archaeologist it appears that no evidence of these things exists, and within British archaeoastronomers any rational discussion concerning the possibility of precision astronomic alignments has become *tabu*. Maybe it is time all this refutation was challenged.

To be sure, there is no perceptible mark, pit or stone hole to mark the 3:2 point of either of the two 5 sides of the rectangle at Stonehenge, nothing tangible that archaeology as practiced today can identify. So not surprisingly, the whole concept described here and in the previous chapter can easily be dismissed as another half-baked theory emerging from the 'lunatic fringe'.

However, this viewpoint will be rendered completely obsolete by the new research presented here that brings a different kind of evidence to the table. Techniques will now be employed to suggest that once there was indeed an intermediate hypotenuse within the Station stone rectangle and that it was being used to further the study of solar and lunar cycles. These techniques combine geometry, astronomy and metrology, i.e. they represent an application of megalithic science.

Evidence for a Lunation Triangle at Stonehenge

The Station stone rectangle provides the basic framework of the construction. It was the earliest linear geometrical construction at Stonehenge after the midsummer sunrise axis had been established alongside the Heel stone, and it will now be assumed that the builders employed a unit length on the rope or rods of 8MY, and were attempting to fabricate an accurate rectangle, of dimensions 40 x 96 MY, whose two diagonals would automatically affirm the squareness of the geometry, and would each be 104 MY long. The likelihood for this to be true has already been discussed (pages 21–25).

Once one understands the mechanism and purpose of the lunation triangle, the length of the intermediate hypotenuse within the Station stone rectangle at Stonehenge can easily be evaluated, and can be readily interpreted in astronomical terms. Its length is 12.369 x 8 = 98.952 MY

To understand why the number 98.95 is so significant, one really has to be an astronomer, or a calendar-designer, and have previous form in studying the way the sun and moon interreact during their eternal journeys along the ecliptic and around the Zodiac. On page 54 and 55 it was seen that this is almost exactly the number of lunations in eight solar years. For a calendar maker, this relationship is a minor miracle - in eight (solar) years, there are almost exactly 99 lunar months. In fact there are 98.946 lunations in eight solar years, and this is the number of megalithic yards in the intermediate hypotenuse of any lunation triangle whose unit length is 8 MY. The accuracy of this repeat cycle is such that the 99th lunation completes just over a day and a half following the end of the eighth (solar) year, an accuracy of 1 part in 1740 (99.943%).

So...in Stonehenge there is a rectangular construction, fabricated in units of 8MY, that enables a 5,12,13 Pythagorean triangle to become a lunation triangle and deliver the number of lunations in eight solar years, that number being almost integer, 99 lunations. Each megalithic yard in this construction thus represents one lunar month, as it naturally might have been expected to, if the original tally count had been in elapsed lunar months. It now becomes possible to now suggest a new purpose for the Station stone rectangle. It appears that one of its purposes was to provide the framework for a lunation triangle, whose intermediate hypotenuse defined a length that corresponded precisely with the number of lunar months in the eight-year soli-lunar repeat cycle. Each of these lunar months is separated on the ground by a distance of one megalithic yard, as the theory predicts (see pages 21-25).

There are other reasons for coming to such a conclusion,

1. The Station stones were set up to align with the extreme solar and lunar rise and set positions. They are shouting "sun!" and "moon!" at anyone conscious enough to observe what is going on in the course of several years at Stonehenge.

2. The Station stone rectangle is aligned with the axis of symmetry of the monument, itself aligned with midsummer and midwinter solar rises and sets. The original axis runs through the centre of the Aubrey circle and the Heel stone is part of this arrangement

3. The Aubrey circle which defines the Station stone rectangle is constructed such that the unit length of the rectangle is 8MY. From the centre of the Aubrey circle to the Heel stone is also dimensioned in 8 MY such that it forms the ratio 12:13 with the diameter of the Aubrey circle.

4. Be they holes, wooden posts or bluestones, the fifty-six markers around the circumference of the Aubrey circle provide, according to Fred Hoyle, one of the most renowned astronomers of the 1960s, the perfect number by which to facilitate an analogue model of the motions of the sun and moon around the Zodiac, and to predict eclipses.

This is a significant step forward in any assessment of what the builders were connecting with when they conceived of and built the Aubrey circle and then the Station stone rectangle. The intermediate hypotenuses of either of the two diagonals may no longer be visible, but their dimensions would have been exactly the correct length to define an 8 year calendar. The whole assemblage is found inside a temple that has, in several other ways, been shown capable of measuring solar and lunar cycles to impressive levels of accuracy. It is not likely that any 3:2 point will be found, repeated excavation of the site has left it, according to Atkinson, 'like a potato patch', following some very dodgy archaeological practices. Perhaps those large Station stones were necessary after all, preserving the message after all the smaller features had been obliterated.

The Cult of the Right-Angled Triangle

Thom showed that Pythagorean triangles had been staked out at many megalithic sites in order for their three corners to provide the centres for radial arcs which would then define the complex perimeter curves of the egg-shaped, elliptical and flattened rings. Once these triangles had performed this task they were then redundant, removed, probably from the moment that perimeter was defined, yet they must once have been pegged out inside that future perimeter, because there is no other simple way to derive those perimeters. Those triangles were constructed solely in order to define and then enable the perimeters of those same rings to be established. Thom identified that these triangles were often constructed with integer side lengths in megalithic yards (or multiples of that unit), just as we have found for the lunation triangle at Stonehenge.

The Station stone rectangle provided the template by which neolithic astronomers could come to understand time reckoning of solar and lunar cycles better and with more accuracy.

A lunar month could and still can be observed and its length determined directly at Stonehenge, by driving the earlier Aubrey circle markers as a detector of solstices, equinoxes, full and new moons (*see page 31, and Heath 1993, 1998, Hoyle 1977*), The length of the solar year can also be tallied from the midsummer/midwinter axis alignment to the northeastern entrance to the henge. Eclipses can be noted, or the transit of a planet by placing a tally or mark at the appropriate place along the intermediate hypotenuse. After the eight-year time period has elapsed this length need be no longer tied to the rectangle, and may be removed off-site and used as an eight year count, perhaps as a component part within the study of longer term astronomical cycles of sun, moon and planets. It could become part of the astronomical history of the observatory monument that was evidently one of the primary functions of Stonehenge, why it was built and why it was built at latitude 51.178°.

The Ideal Megalithic Observatory Site

Where would this celestial history be laid out and studied? A long and sheltered flat field would be essential for astronomical analysis when using long ropes as the storage medium. Marked up year-ropes could be laid out end-on-end and their astronomical timings, such as eclipses and planetary standstills or transits seen as a linear pattern. The rope lengths and their tally marks could readily be copied, the 'recording' passed on to other communities or stored for future use. Two examples of ideal locations for such activities are to be found immediately north of Stonehenge, almost within a stone's throw. The first construction is the

Stonehenge cursus, some 1.9 miles long. Estimates for its construction date it prior to the first stages of Stonehenge, at around 3500 BC. Its purpose is presently unknown. The second construction is the later Stonehenge avenue, stretching nearly 2000 feet in the direction of the midsummer sunrise before veering off to the right, down to the river Avon. The avenue is currently dated contemporarily with the building of the larger sarsen constructions, around 2600 BC. The avenue is presently thought to be a processional walkway to the monument from nearby Durrington Walls and Woodhenge.

Stonehenge is truly wonderful, but it is also, more or less, a badly damaged and well-eroded ruin, yet through the efforts of archaeologists, astronomers and various members of the lunatic fringe, it has begun to reveal some of its secrets. One of these is the lunation triangle, a device that enabled the neolithic astronomers to store and transfer astronomical knowledge. This was a form of writing for a culture becoming ever more conscious of the connections between the the sky and the earth. My next quest was to find other surviving examples of this device - which I did.

Stonehenge has always provided a focus of interest for travellers and tourists alike. This 1728 engraving appears to depict a 'Special Access' tour of the period.

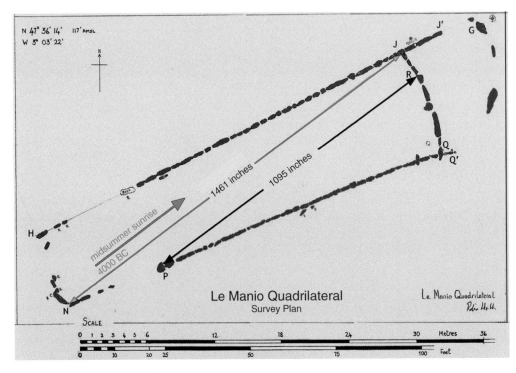

N 47° 36' 14'   117' AMSL
W 5° 03' 22'

1461 inches

1095 inches

midsummer sunrise
4000 BC

H

N

P

J

J'

G

R

Q

Q'

Le Manio Quadrilateral
Survey Plan

Le Manio Quadrilateral
Robin Heath

SCALE

| 0 | 1 | 2 | 3 | 4 | 5 | 6 | 12 | 18 | 24 | 30 | Metres | 36 |

| 0 | 10 | 20 | 25 | 50 | 75 | 100 | Feet |

Chapter Five

Finding other Lunation Triangles

The theory behind the lunation triangle originated from original survey work around Stonehenge and Avebury undertaken during the late 1980s and early 1990s. At that time the two remaining stones of the station rectangle, and the 5:12 rectangle they and their two missing companions defined, provided the only known and seemingly nebulous example of a possible device. What was clearly needed were more examples of the *genre*, preferably which had survived in a more complete and rather better condition than had the Station stone rectangle. Such a find could provide more solid evidence of human intent underpinning their structure.

My journey to fully understand the implications of this device has taken until now (January 2014) and in that time no less than three other surviving examples have been found. The first two of of these is described in this chapter, the third example is the *Proto Stonehenge*, the subject of this book, and it has a chapter all to itself.

The Le Manio Quadrilateral

A lunation triangle was identified in Brittany in the midsummer of 2009, during a conference organised by a local institution, ACEM. The quadrilateral is found alongside a pathway near a small hamlet called Le Manio, to the east of the main Carnac alignments. It is very early, being dated prior to 3500 BC. The site takes the form of an almost contiguous quadrilateral of stones, most of which have survived in good condition. During the following year I undertook a theodolite survey of the site with my brother Richard, reproduced on page sixty five. Thom undertook a very basic survey of the site in 1974, and linked it to a large menhir (stone L) placed near to Le Menec stone ring at the western end of the long alignments (*Megalithic remains in Britain and Brittany*, Oxford, 1978).

In 2008 a local researcher, Howard Crowhurst, fortunately produced a theodolite survey of the entire Le Manio complex, without which it is unlikely that the lunation triangle hidden within the quadrilateral would have been discovered. Crowhurst's original survey revealed the existence of both 3,4,5 and 5,12,13 triangles connecting the various monuments of this complex site together (*see opposite*). These triangles employed integer units of either the MY or the megalithic rod (2.5 MY). This significant research showed that the technology used in Carnac was basically similar to that employed in the construction of Stonehenge, and that the megalithic science was already in place before 3500 BC. The builders of Le Manio were developing the earliest known precision geometrically based astronomy on the planet.

Although I had previously (2009) identified that the quadrilateral was, from its dimensions, recording days using a scale of four inches/day, it was Richard who later picked his way through my survey report and identified that day-inch counting had been employed and that this device was built to record three solar years, the intermediate hypotenuse being 1096 inches in length (3 x 365.2422 inches). It is unlikely that this discovery would ever have been picked up by surveyors using the metre.

During March 2010, a fuller survey undertaken by both Richard and myself revealed this to be the case, and also revealed that both a three and four year count was being operated from the same site using a structure based on a 'four-square' geometry (a three by twelve rectangle), effectively a sawn-off lunation triangle. In addition, as if to confirm the function of the site, the diagonals of each rectangle were aimed directly at the midsummer sunrise in around 4000 BC

Day-inch counting was seen by Richard Heath to provide insights into the methodology and chronology of the megalithic culture. In metrology, for instance, the three-year soli-lunar repeat cycle adds up, numerically to supply a possible source for the origin of the megalithic yard. Three yearly overflows of 10.875 days, as inches, accrue to 32.655 inches, the overflow has then become the length of the megalithic yard, 32.655 inches is, in feet, 2.7188 ft.

The full survey report on Le Manio is currently available free as a PDF on www.skyandlandscape. com, there is also more material on www.megalithic science.org).

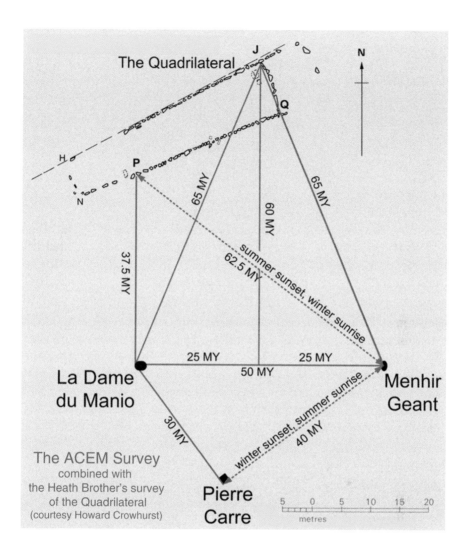

The ACEM Survey
combined with
the Heath Brother's survey
of the Quadrilateral
(courtesy Howard Crowhurst)

The Preseli-Stonehenge Landscape Triangle

In 1991, I noticed that Stonehenge was located exactly east of the centre of Lundy Island, a small island in the Bristol Channel itself located south of the Bluestone region of the Preselis. The resulting right angle, at Lundy *centre ville*, framed a large and accurate 5,12,13 triangle whose hypotenuse connected the Preselis and their bluestones to Stonehenge. The dimensions of this triangle were numerically related to those of the Station stone rectangle. The scaling is 2500:1, making this triangle a very large undertaking indeed. And Caldey Island, just off the coast near Tenby, provided a perfect 3:2 point! But is this triangle real, or merely a *chimera*?

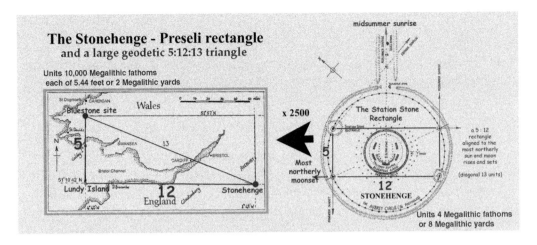

Although there may be some small leeway in the dimensions above, for reasons already discussed earlier here relating to the size of the larger triangle, if this geodetic form is to be considered as deriving from human intent, that alone would make 100% accuracy almost impossible. Yet almost such an accuracy is found in a triangle defined by locating corners at Stonehenge (centre), Lundy (centre) and the trig point on the summit of Carn Wen, near the neolithic settlement around Glandy Cross in the Preselis. The illustration above shows the triangle, and here are its main specifications,

1. At the centre of Lundy Island, just north of the spring fed 'flash' lake, is a raised area whose summit is exactly west of Stonehenge. From this can be seen the Preseli hills, due north, and at night, the lighthouse flashing its regular beat from the southern tip of Caldey Island. With a theodolite it is possible to establish that the bluestone outcrops on Carn Meini are almost directly north. In a huge geodetic form that turns out to also be very closely dimensioned in its side lengths to a 5,12,13 Pythagorean triangle, the centre of Lundy Island acts as the right angle.

2. The triangle is aligned with the cardinal directions.

3. The dimensions of this triangle are almost exactly 100,000, 240,000 and 260,000 megalithic yards in length.

4. The unit length is 20,000 megalithic yards, making the scale 2,500:1, compared with the Station stone rectangle.

5. Caldey Island, just off the coast at Tenby, supplies a suitable 3:2 point on the shortest 'five' side of the triangle as it tracks northwards towards the Preselis. This is historically satisfying.

6. The '13' side of this triangle connects the Preseli region to Stonehenge directly, at 133 miles distant.

7. Replicating a rectangle 2500 times larger than the Station stone rectangle places the northern right-hand corner at Eyford Park, near Temple Guiting, and a second 3:2 point can be located *en route* between Temple Guiting and Stonehenge, at the Iron age site of Barbury Castle, near Avebury, Wiltshire.

8. Lundy, Caldey and the Preseli main ridge are natural locations arranged such that they align along a north-south line. Stonehenge, on the other hand, is a man-made construction. In the previous section the rectangular arrangement between extreme sun and moon rises and sets has been shown to be aligned with the Station stone rectangle and this can only be observed within about twenty miles of the latitude of Stonehenge. The giant geodetic rectangle therefore provides an explanation for the choice of the location of Stonehenge, as the southeastern 'corner' of this construction, connecting it through the geometry of the lunation triangle with the Preseli bluestone region. Otherwise there is, as yet, no other explanation.

It has not yet been possible to positively identify this construct with prehistoric provenance, any more than archaeologists have been able to affirm that the bluestones arrived at Stonehenge through the action of human intent. The matter remains one of probabilities. The bluestones employed in the construction of Stonehenge are immediately tangible, the huge triangle much less so, such that it appears to be an abstracted form. But its dimensions, ratios and units of length offer a wealth of detail supporting the view that it is more than a *chimera*, much more than an imaginative fantasy of the author. However, proof it appears not to offer, and other examples are needed, and were sought after.

The outcome from work at Le Manio substantiated knowledge of the lunation triangle's function within the megalithic culture of northwestern Europe. Stonehenge became no longer unique in containing the potential for such a device. After eighteen years of searching, a third and almost complete lunation triangle had been found. But I still wanted to discover more evidence that the 'potential' lunation triangle at Stonehenge was a tangible geometrical device. During the long hot summer of 2013 a fourth example was discovered much nearer home, in bluestone country, the Preseli region of West Wales. It was found to be related to the Station stone rectangle at Stonehenge. The following chapters tell the story of a significant discovery, one that I have named *the Carningli triangle*.

Proto Stonehenge in Wales

Above: Carningli summit from Glanrhyd. Below: Crugiau Cemaes from Glanrhyd. Opposite: Llech y Drybedd.

Chapter Six

The Carningli Triangle

In the summer of 2013, while undertaking a survey from Carningli summit on another matter, a large geodetic 5,12,13 triangle was revealed, spread across the rural landscape of West Wales between Carningli and Moylegrove, within the Pembrokeshire National Park. At the time I could not believe that I had never previously recognised it. The Carningli triangle provides the principal subject of this chapter, and is directly connected to the Station stone rectangle at Stonehenge and its 'inner' lunation triangle. The two constructions can be shown to be linked through their integrated astronomy, geometry and metrology, and are clearly the result of identical cultural impulses. The Carningli triangle is therefore a *Proto-Stonehenge*, and the main subject of this book.

The three sites which define the corners of the triangle's geometry are illustrated in the three photographs on this spread.

Finding Welsh Gold - A Right Welsh Triangle

The Carningli triangle was identified early in July 2013 and subsequently surveyed during the last six months of 2013. Located a few miles north of the bluestone outcrops that jut out along the main ridge or spine of the Preseli range of hills, each of the triangle's three corners is defined by a well-known and classified prehistoric site. There is public access to each of the component sites. Only when the locations of these three 'corner' sites are joined up to present a triangular form can the full extent of what they represent be appreciated.

In addition to the three corner sites, there is a significant standing stone that provides additional evidence to confirm the function of the triangle and which helps in identifying the design processes that were employed during its construction. From surveys undertaken at this and several other standing stones elsewhere in the vicinity, it became clear that the Carningli triangle once formed part of a much larger landscape pattern.

Within the megalithic landscape of coastal West Wales this artifact represents an astonishingly rich new source of information concerning the capabilities of the culture that once constructed monuments here, and later, at Stonehenge. It can be demonstrated that this artifact shares many of its most significant characteristics with the astronomy, geometry and metrology of the Station stone rectangle at Stonehenge.

In other words: *there is a cultural connection between these two monuments in their design requirements and processes, demonstrating that they both derive from the same cultural origins.*

THE THREE SITES
A Triangle for All Seasons

Location One
CARNINGLI
Latitude 51N°59' 59.00"   Longitude 4W°49' 26.32"   Elevation 1049'

Carningli summit (CI) provides the first location of the triangle, its 'sharp end'. A small but level platform immediately below the summit consists of a diminutive slab of rock set level within the chaotic jumble of volcanic rocks once spewed out from the summit during Carningli's active period, about 100 million years ago. This corner location resembles a small throne, facing to the northeast, where, on the horizon can be seen Cemaes Head, seven miles away. Seventy feet to the northeast of this location is an alternative location similarly set up to enable observations to the other two corners while offering protection from the elements to the observers. Sited in part of the remains of the 'fort' that has been variously described as originating from the Iron Age, Bronze Age and Neolithic in books written over the past fifty years, this alternative location has also been analysed as the possible corner of the triangle on Carningli summit.

The 'Throne' on Carningli summit. The level seat is directed towards Llech y Drybedd, but also provides a backsight to a spectacular solar alignment via the pointed cairn visible here on the horizon. On February 18th the sun sets into an 'egg-cup' (*marked above*) formed by two distant conical outcrops (Carn Llidi and Penberi) near St Davids.*

On intermediate high ground at a range of around four and half miles can be seen two very well known prehistoric sites, each of high archaeological calibre, and both visible to the naked eye from either Carningli location. Recognised as Neolithic and/or Bronze Age sites, these sites provide the second and third 'corners' that define the artifact.

A little warning: Carningli is an exposed site over 1000 feet above sea level and it can become quite difficult to navigate over the treacherous rocky terrain when it is either windy or wet, or both, a common occurrence in West Wales. If you are planning a walk to the summit, take the normal precautions required for any hill walk, warm clothing, suitable footwear, some food and drink, a map and compass or GPS. Watch the weather!

(* See appendix ten.)

Looking south over Llech y Drybedd towards Pentre Ifan, Cwmcerwyn and the main Preseli ridge. The outcrops of Carnedd Meibion Owen can be seen above the capstone on the intermediate horizon. The magnificent setting for this dolmen is matched only by the astonishing properties this site has revealed during the past 25 years of research.

Location Two

LLECH Y DRYBEDD

Lat 52N°03′ 16.30″   Long 4W°46′ 18.10″   Elevation 619′

Llech y Drybedd (LYD) provides the second location in the geometrical construction being revealed. One mile west of the rural village of Moylegrove, this large dolmen has previously been shown to contain as its 'cargo' a stunningly visual midsummer sunset alignment to Lughnaquilla mountain, 93 miles away in Co. Wicklow in Ireland [Illus and website]. Llech y Drybedd is closely aligned north of Pentre Ifan, part of an north-south alignment that stretches across Cardigan Bay to distant Bardsey Island. There is also a precision lunar alignment to the most northerly moonset from a nearby henge site later employed as an early Christian burial site, called simply Y Gaer. [Visit www.skyandlandscape.com website for more details, and read *Bluestone Magic* (2010, Bluestone Press and Llanerch Press].

Location Three
CRUGIAU CEMAES
Lat 52N° 02′ 27.86″   Long 4W° 44′ 05.35″   Elevation 619′

Crugiau Cemaes (CC) provides the third site in the construction. Once comprising three tumuli arranged in a row running southwest to northeast (at an azimuth of 20 degrees), the middle tump became a storage reservoir, used until 2011, and the two others have been excavated. The most northerly tumulus, and highest point on the site, contains an Ordnance Survey triangulation point.

Prominently sited on a natural hilltop, Crugiau Cemaes may be found two and a half miles east of Nevern on the B4582 road. It is the local highest spot and offers perhaps the best view of the Preseli coastal region to be had anywhere. Crugiau Cemaes is visible from many other sites within the Preselis and can even be seen from Aberystwyth, over forty miles distant. I have seen its characteristic multiple tumps from Bardsey Island, which is located almost directly north at a range of fifty miles.

For years a cast-iron information board informed the visitor to this well known viewpoint that the prehistoric cairns were constructed in the Bronze Age, and the site was dated then at around 1600 BC, the normal dating in vogue sixty years ago. The sign vanished some years back as it needed to. A more recent interpretation board has also since vanished.

Looking southeast from Llech y Drybedd to Crugiau Cemaes. The middle tump was a concrete reservoir until 2011. The trig point can be seen on the summit of the left hand tump, and this location defines the third corner point of the Carningli triangle.

All three of these sites are therefore located on high ground and the survey revealed a previously unrecognised geometric relationship between them. Connecting three sites together will always create a triangle of course, but this turned out to be no ordinary triangle. It is accurately a right angled triangle, a very unexpected first property which led on to a second surprise: the three side lengths form the integer ratios 5, 12 and 13 to each other. A 5,12,13 'Pythagorean' triangle is formed between three prominent prehistoric sites in the Preseli region of West Wales. The geometry is so accurately defined that it cannot be an accidental coincidence.

Defining the Accuracy

To determine just how true the geometry of the triangle is, one must measure it accurately. How 'right' is the right angle, for example, and are the two acute angles accurately those of a 5,12,13 triangle? What are the lengths of the three sides?

The triangle is small enough to be considered as a two dimensional construction. Spherical distortion caused by the earth's curvature on plane or two-dimensional geometry causes the sum of the three internal angles of the triangle angles to exceed 180°. This angular expansion is negligable on any geodetic or landscape polygon if its dimensions are less than about twenty miles in length, and, not surprisingly, this example's angular total lies within 0.13 degrees of 180°.

Using a good optical surveying theodolite it was possible to determine the three internal angles to an accuracy of better than one minute of one degree. The results are shown below in Tables One and Two. The angles alone show how well the triangle conforms to an ideal 5,12,13 triangle

ANALYSIS OF THE CARNINGLI TRIANGLE

The internal angles of an 'ideal' 5,12,13 triangle are 22.619°, 67.381° and 90°. In DMS format these angles are 22° 37' 11", 67° 22' 49" and 90°. Only if all three angles of the triangle hold these values can each of the triangle's three sides fall exactly in the correct proportion with its neighbours and the triangle shape up to form a perfect 5,12,13 ratio. This would represent the ideal form of the 5,12,13, to be compared in any analysis with the reality achieved on the ground during any practical attempt to recreate the ideal triangle, as measured with modern surveying equipment.

All practical attempts at fabricating such a triangle on the ground will incur various inaccuracies, both in angular and dimensional integrity. These minute differences from the ideal can be evaluated, and there are several different ways the lengths and angles can be measured. These are presented in Table One, on page 76.

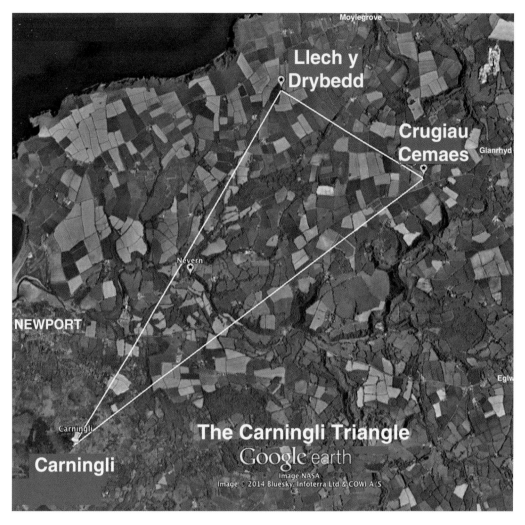

The Carningli Triangle

The Carningli triangle is shown above. The right angle at Llech y Drybedd is 99.66% accurate, the smaller of the other two angles, which should be 22.619°, measures 22.58° with a theodolite, which is 99.82% accurate. The larger of the other two angles measures 67.76°, when the ideal would be 67.38°, so the measured angle is larger than the ideal, with an accuracy of 99.5%. This is accurate enough to confirm the triangle was built as a 5,12,13 geodetic structure.

All three side lengths can be determined as distances when the distance between any two corners has been measured, either by employing pythagoras' theorem, or by using basic trigonometry. Various methods for measuring the side are used in the analysis, but Google Earth gives side lengths of 9647 feet, 23,136 feet and 25070 feet. The unit length of the triangle is 1928.4 feet.

Proto Stonehenge in Wales

The angles of the Carningli triangle have an accuracy above 99.6% in all but one case. One of the Google Earth derived angles, which is defining an angle near to the steep slope that runs up the northeastern flank of Carningli, is distorted. The overall angular resolution of the triangle attains better than one part in 2,500, about eight minutes of one degree. This falls well within the accepted limit for naked eye resolution over the distances involved. These angles are accurate, so one can be sure that a 5,12,13 triangle was intended. How these angles may have been defined will be covered in a later section, defined they certainly were, and accurately so.

TABLE ONE

ANGULAR MEASUREMENTS OF THE CARNINGLI TRIANGLE

1.Azimuth angles obtained from a theodolite. (Theodolite - Wild T16)
[angles obtained from a sun-shoot)
Azimuth of LYD from CI   =   30° 27′ 00″
Azimuth of CI from CC   = 233° 08′ 30″
Azimuth of LYD from CC = 300° 31′ 00″

2. Internal angles of the triangle calculated from azimuth angles above,

Data	Measured	Error
Internal angle at LYD	= 90° 04′ 00″	+4′ 00″ (99.926%)
Internal angle at CC	= 67° 22′ 29″	zero (100%)
Internal angle at CI	= 22° 41′ 30″	+4′ 19″(99.682%)

3. Direct theodolite measurements of the internal angles
(Theodolite - Wild T16)

Data	Measured	Error
Angle 1. Theodolite at LYD; CI to CC,	= 89°54′57″	5′ 43″ (99.910%)
Angle 2. Theodolite at CC; LYD to CI,	= 67°23′06″	0′ 17″ (99.993%
Angle 3. Theodolite at CI; CC to LYD,	= 22°41′56″	4′ 45″ (99.650%)

[The ideal angles of a 5, 12, 13 triangle are 22° 37′ 11″, 67° 22′ 49″ and 90° 00′ 00].

76

Measuring the Lengths of the Three Sides of the Triangle

There are two main ways by which the lengths of the three sides of a geodetic right-angled triangle may be evaluated. The first is through the traditional longhand calculations based on the latitude and longitude coordinates of each pair of sites. These calculations give a point-to-point distance between any two sites, taking no account of the intermediate terrain. They assume that all the points are located on a plane or two-dimensional surface. The results are given in Table Two below together with the relevant bearing angle or azimuth of the line drawn between each pair of sites.

The second method is to use satellite imagery. Google Earth offers a direct and rapid measurement over ground from point to point around the triangle, together with the azimuth angles and elevation (height) above mean sea level. Google Earth assumes that the planet is almost spherical and consequently, over long distances (above 10 miles) these angles will change significantly from those that would have been obtained from plane surveying and which must be accounted for when appropriate. The dimensions of the Carningli triangle fall well below the point where this distortion becomes significant.

To make this point clearer, the largest difference between the two calculation methods is between Carningli and Llech y Drybedd, at one part in 380, the other two are 1 in 1500 (Carningli and Crugiau Cemaes) and 1 in 536 (Llech y Drybedd to Crugiau Cemaes).

TABLE TWO

THE METROLOGY OF THE CARNINGLI TRIANGLE

Coordinates of latitude and Longitude

Carningli	Lat 51°N 59' 59"	4W 49' 26" Elevation 1049'
Llech y Drybedd	Lat 52°N 03' 16"	4W 46' 18" Elevation 619'
Crugiau Cemaes	Lat 52°N 02' 28"	4W 44' 06" Elevation 619'

(WGS84. Garmin eTrex GPS navigator and Google Earth)

The Side Lengths of the Triangle

1. Longhand Calculation of side lengths from above coordinates

Carningli to Llech y Drybedd ('12' side) = 23,197 ft,   Az 30°25'53"

Carningli to Crugiau Cemaes ('13' side) = 25086 ft,   Az 53°01'06"

Llech y Drybedd to Crugiau ('5' side)   = 9629 feet,   Az 30°39'38"

UNIT LENGTH

The perimeter around the triangle is,

9629 + 23,197.0 + 25,086 = 57912.3feet,

The perimeter divided by 30 gives the unit length as 1930.41 feet.

2. Measured 'over ground' using Google Earth

Carningli to Llech y Drybedd ('12' side) = 23,136 ft,   Az 30°22'12"

Carningli to Crugiau Cemaes ('13' side) = 25070 ft,   Az 53°00'10"

Llech y Drybedd to Crugiau ('5' side)   = 9647 feet, Az 300°36'00"

UNIT LENGTH

The perimeter around the triangle is,

9647 + 23,136.0 + 25070 = 57853 feet,

The perimeter divided by 30 gives the unit length as 1928.43 feet.

3. Measured 'over ground', (Google Earth)

(the alternative Carningli site)

Coordinates of latitude and Longitude

Alternative Carningli site   Lat 51°N 59' 59.57"   4W 49' 25.78" Elev: 1049'

Carningli to Llech y Drybedd ('12' side) = 23,148.70 ft, Az 30°25'11"

Carningli to Crugiau Cemaes ('13' side) = 25078.54 ft, Az 53°05'24"

Llech y Drybedd to Crugiau ('5' side)   = 9645.89 ft, Az 300°35'00"

UNIT LENGTH

The perimeter around the triangle is,

9645.89 + 23,148.7 + 25078.54 = 57873.13 feet,

The perimeter divided by 30 gives the unit length as 1929.1043 feet.

TABLE THREE
ANGLES DERIVED FROM THE SIDE LENGTHS OF THE TRIANGLE

1. Internal angles derived from side lengths

Data	Measured	Error
Angle 1. From CI to CC,	= 89°54′17″	5′ 43″ (99.894%)
Angle 2. From LYD to CI,	= 67°32′00″	9′ 11″ (99.773%)
Angle 3. From CC to LYD, [180* [180 - (angle 1+ angle 2)]	= 22°33′42″	3′ 29″ (99.743%)

2. Satellite Imagery derived values for the internal angles of the triangle.

Data	Measured	Error
Angle 1. From CI to CC,	= 89°41′24″	18′ 55″ (99.650%)
Angle 2. From LYD to CI,	= 67°44′24″	21′ 35″ (99.466%)
Angle 3. From CC to LYD,	= 22°34′12″	02′ 59″ (99.780%)

[The ideal angles of a 5, 12, 13 triangle are 22° 37′ 11″, 67° 22′ 49″ and 90° 00′ 00].

Adjustment of the Corner Locations

The terrain over which the three sides of the Carningli triangle run contains steep sided and often forested valleys, making the establishment of direct measurement of all the lengths of the triangle a highly improbable and daunting prospect, especially to the accuracy obtained in Tables One and Two. So how was the triangle defined?

There is a clue. All three corner locations are located on hill-top ridges, and significantly the long ridge of Carningli summit lies approximately at the same angle as does the direction of Llech y Drybedd. The ridge upon which Llech y Drybedd is located similarly allows some movement of this monument in order to obtain the required right angle between Carn Ingli and Crugiau Cemaes. Finally, the ridge upon which the three cairns of Crugiau Cemaes have been built roughly aligns with the direction to Carningli.

This makes all three corner points somewhat adjustable in length in order to 'fine-tune' the required angles in order to furnish an accurate 5,12,13 triangle. From these angles the triangle's side lengths follow, in the correct ratios, but with no likely possibility for a predetermined or preferred unit of length. The shape will be correct, the side lengths will form the ratio 5,12,13 to each other, but the unit of length will be whatever it turns out to be – in this triangle it is within a foot of being 1929 feet (588m), whichever measurement technique is employed (*see Table Two*).

FINDING THE UNIT LENGTH
Two Methods to Establish the Unit Length

A twenty-first century researcher investigating a triangle constructed over five millenia ago possesses several advantages over his predecessors, the principal one being the availability of satellite imagery via the internet. This triangle can be measured using whichever of several modern techniques that are available, and analysed using any one of the various methods now to be described.

The best estimate of the unit of length of this complex artifact can be determined by carefully measuring the perimeter length around the entire triangle, and then dividing that length by thirty (5 + 12 + 13 = 30) to find the average unit length. If the triangle were shown to employ a unit of length that was metrologically and / or astronomically significant, then this would indicate a higher level of skill on the part of the builders. Knowing the unit length accurately provides a crucial piece of evidence enabling a researcher to establish the intentions, knowledge and capabilities of the original architect-surveyors.

Another method would be to measure one side length, and then evaluate the other two side lengths found by using Pythagoras's theorem or basic trigonometry. Division of the total perimeter length by 30 would then establish the unit length as described above, but would be based on a single measurement only, thereby less accurate than incorporating the fundamental measurements of all the side lengths.

One traditional method, pre-satellite and pre-GPS, would be to establish a known length as a base-line some distance from one side of the triangle, and then measure the angles to the corner positions from its ends using a good theodolite, a calculation which would supply the required length of that side of the triangle, and which would take weeks.

A second traditional technique would involve taking the coordinates of latitude and longitude for each pair of sites in turn and calculating their distance apart. Table Two shows this technique to reveal a unit length of 1930.4 feet.

The task is quickest done in modern times by measuring just the shortest side length, determined to be 9647 feet, by 'mousing' a Google Earth track between Llech y Drybedd and Crugiau Cemaes, the 'five' side of the Carningli triangle, and then dividing this length by five. The result is a length of 1929.1 feet, obtained in a couple of minutes.

Better still would be take ten minutes longer to employ this same technique on all three sides, the triangle then found to have a unit length of 1928. 4 feet (the difference between all these techniques is very small, less than nine inches in 1929 feet or one part in 2755).

If any of these ways of determining the unit length turn out to produce a length having no apparent metrological or astronomical significance, then this might suggest that the method employed to define the triangle was to first define its internal angles, method one above. The 5,12,13 ratio is obtained but there will be no likely significance in the lengths themselves. If however the unit length possessed significance, the construction must have involved the measurement of lengths between one or more of the component sites.

The unit lengths from both methods of calculation of all three lengths are shown in Table Two. These unit lengths are 1930.4, 1928.4 or 1929.1 feet. Later on in this analysis it will be necessary to return to the unit length in order to determine whether this has metrological and/or astronomical significance.

A Synthesis of Astronomy, Geometry and Metrology

The angular and linear accuracy of the triangle catalogued in tables one, two and three could only have been achieved by a sophisticated culture. The lingering stereotype of Neolithic Britons struggling for survival, praying for death or civilisation to come and rescue them from their wretchedness, withers beneath the unfolding display of geodetic expertise that has been revealed. The analysis reveals that these three sites do indeed form an accurate 5,12,13 triangle. But there is something else that can be determined from this form, suggesting where the astronomy of the lunation triangle could have originated.

The Astronomy of the Carningli Triangle

It is hard to believe that people in the Neolithic period, whom we have been told were predominently farmers, did not recognise that the length of the seasonal year was related to the sun's height in the sky and that the way the day: night ratio varied throughout the year was cyclical, and that the yearly round was a recurrent cycle. Evidence from the astronomical qualities of the monuments in the Preseli region has determined that this was familiar territory, and more. Proof of this fact lies all around the Carningli triangle and is even built into its corners.

For example, Llech y Drybedd is a beautifully crafted dolmen site that contains many astronomical features within its structure and location. Its capstone is unusually chunky, and its axis of symmetry points to that point on the horizon where the midsummer sun sets. The flat top of the capstone slopes downwards to face the sunset. Looking adjacent to the dolmen, along the '12' side of the Carningli triangle, the capstone mirrors the summit of Carningli, something commented on in many archaeology books. In truth, there is a right angle built into the shape of the rear of the capstone, and now that the dolmen's role in the Carningli triangle has been revealed, other 'mirroring' aspects of the capstone leap out of the monument's structure and offer visual clues concerning the function of the site within the larger triangle (*see photographs below and opposite*).

The solar solstitial alignment to Ireland has already been discussed (*see appendix and www.skyandlandscape.com*), as has the major standstill moonset from nearby Gaer to the monument, where Llech y Drybedd

provides the foresight. The minor lunar standstill can similarly be observed from Crugiau Cemaes, again with Llech y Drybedd providing the foresight.

The precise St David's alignment (*see appendix and www.skyandlandscape.com*) and the solstitial alignment from Llech y Drybedd would have given assurances that the year was consistently 365 days in length and that the most northerly sunset always occurred at the same extreme northern horizon point at midsummer. The backsight for this alignment is the 'throne' described earlier, the corner of the triangle on the ridge of Carningli summit. And from a large flat stone beneath Pentre Ifan, the capstone of the monument marks an intermediate foresight for the midwinter solstice sunset down the right-hand side of the most southerly of the Carnedd Meibion Owen outcrops (*see www. skyandlandscape.com*).

The 18.6 year nodal cycle of the moon could also be evaluated and monitored using Llech y Drybedd as a foresight from either Y Gaer (major standstill) or Crugiau Cemaes (minor standstill) and viewing alternatively the setting moon at a major and then a minor standstill, every 9.3 years. This would immediately determine the two (opposite) months in the year when eclipses can occur (*see appendix twelve, page 108*).

Everything needed to observe and accurately record the key cycles of the sun and moon was already in place at Llech y Drybedd, around

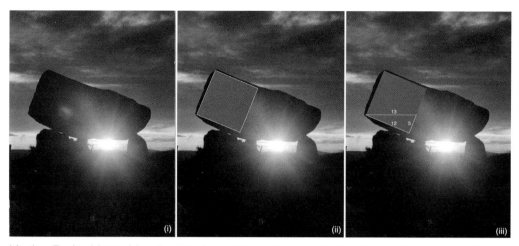

Llech y Drybedd provides the location of the right angle in the Carningli triangle, and once this is revealed, one can then enjoy the above playful visual clues as to its role, provided by the shape and angle of tilt of its capstone. The triptych above shows the midwinter sunset at the dolmen, the photograph below is the story of the function of the monument, once one knows about the Carningli triangle. It does precisely what it says on the capstone.

2850 BC, the present date of construction according to archaeologists. The site is perfectly set up to observe and evaluate the key astronomical constants of both the sun and moon. The triangle could have emerged from a few extremely able and intuitive astronomers following on from the astronomical observations that the evidence here suggests were taking place in West Wales during the Neolithic period.

Analysis of the Metrology of the Carningli 5,12,13 Triangle

The archaeological dating of this triangle is closely comparable with the construction date for the Station stone rectangle. The Stonehenge Station stone rectangle employed 8 MY as the unit length. If one applies this same unit length to the sides of the Carningli triangle, the following is obtained, (*figures calculated from each of the three techniques listed in Table Two*).

TABLE FOUR

Side lengths in units of 8 MY
(*each unit represents one day*)

	5 side	12 side	13 side
Longhand	442.18	1062.45	1152.00
Google Earth (i)	443.01	1065.26	1151.27
Google Earth (ii)	442.96	1063.00	1151.66
Astronomical period	15 months	36 months	39 months

From whichever data source, these numbers all closely approximate to the number of days in 15, 36 and 39 lunar months, which are 442.96, 1063.10 and 1151.69 days respectively. To determine the side lengths as lunar months the numbers above must be divided, as days, by the period of the lunar month, 29.53059 days. Either of the locations on Carningli summit produce the same unexpected and highly significant result, for they multiply by three the number ratios of the triangle, five, twelve and thirteen. The fractional components are very small, the triangle is near-integer from any one of the data sets supplied, and this reveals three important things,

a). It reveals a 'hidden' astronomical component within the triangle's dimensions and this could not have come about by accident. The triangle's lengths were planned and then measured out, in units of 8MY.

b). It supports the use of the time unit 'lunar months' found within the Station stone rectangle at Stonehenge, whose unit length is also 8 megalithic yards.

c). It suggests that the Carningli triangle was designed to record lunar months in its side lengths.

d). The '12' side length is intended to represent three lunar years. Each division of the '12' side is one unit length, established by accurate measurement as being 1929.1043 feet. This length must therefore represent three lunar months or lunations.

3 x 354.367 days = 1063 days [3 lunar years]

36 x 29.53059 = 1063.1 days [36 lunar months]

It is something special to discover an accurate 5,12,13 triangle built during the Neolithic period, this alone connects the construction with Stonehenge, through the geometry of the Station stone rectangle. But it is quite something else when its side lengths record elapsed lunar months, in days, using the very same length of 8MY as found at Stonehenge. The Carningli triangle employs 8MY to represent one day, while at Stonehenge the same length was used represent a lunar month. The Carningli triangle is therefore astronomically 'live', and its side lengths are familiar in the same astronomical context as were those comprising the Station stone rectangle. Here is an embarrassment of riches, certainly enough to lever the archaeological model of prehistory off onto a whole new track.

It would be quite exceptional to now discover an associated intermediate hypotenuse making this construction a lunation triangle. Such a discovery would then provide the accurate integration of lunar months within the framework of the solar year, or multiples of the year. It is readily possible to calculate the length of the intermediate hypotenuse, from Google Earth or by applying trigonometry from the other three side lengths. Taking the longest '13' side, at 25078.54 ft, this must be multiplied by 12.369/13 in order to determine the length, which measures in at exactly 23861.27 ft in length.

25078.54 x 12.369/13 = 23,861.27 ft

In units of 8 MY, the intermediate hypotenuse is 1095.76 units long, the length of three solar years (1095.73 days), to within one hour.

1095.73 (days) x 8 x 2.722 ft = 23,860.54 ft,

This corresponds with the length measured directly from the map. The Carningli triangle was clearly intended to be a lunation triangle that recorded three solar years, each day being represented by 8 megalithic yards. The accuracy is astonishing, making its function crystal clear.

This is very strong evidence to support that the Carningli triangle was a three-year counting device used to observe and record solar and lunar events. But there is other solid evidence of an intermediate hypotenuse having been attached to this 5,12,13 triangle. The method by which the

Carningli triangle became a lunation triangle can still be found on the ground, if one knows what to look for.

Evidence for an Intermediate Hypotenuse and the 3:2 point

On the far side of a field adjacent to the B4582 Cardigan to Nevern road stands the well classified Trefael stone, a near semi-circular standing stone peppered with cup and ring marks. The stone has, in recent times, its own website, and it stands in a field near Dryslwyn farm. Its survival has preserved, through its location alone, the method by which the 3:2 point was determined.

The Trefael Stone

The Trefael stone's location is
N 52° 01′ 42″ ; W 4° 46′ 01″ (WGS84)

Located on private land, the stone can be seen from a gate which allows a view through the tall hedge bounding the B4582 road. The stone is some distance from a footpath that runs through the edge of the field within which the stone has stood since prehistoric times. The stone has a large presence and there is a fine view to Carningli.

The Trefael stone

The Trefael (or sometimes *Trefoel*) stone may once have been the capstone of a dolmen. Located on private land it is necessary to seek permission from the local landowner to approach the stone. The photograph shows the semi-circular form of the stone, which is inscribed with various cup and ring marks. Various websites provide hundreds of useful images of the stone within its local landscape, with customary archaeological interpretation. If there was ever a message contained within all the cup marks, it continues to elude modern man. However, the stone's location alone provides all the message one requires to indicate how the 3:2 point of the Carningli triangle came to be placed.

The builders of the Carningli triangle could have measured the length of the '5' side of their big triangle, and somehow divided this into five, then placed the resulting rope three times along the route of the '5' side to the desired point. But they do not appear to have done this, perhaps they could not use numbers or divide in the way we do.

Everything so far employed in this analysis was accomplished with geometry and lengths of ropes, and at Trefael we find the same techniques being employed. What the architects of this triangle do appear to have done was to create a large 3,4,5 Pythagorean triangle from Llech y Drybedd, using the identical unit length to that already used in the Carningli triangle. This supposition can be confirmed because, fortunately, they left behind some of their working hardware and their method of using it.

The shortest side of the Carningli triangle construction (the '5' side from Crugiau Cemaes to Llech y Drybedd) was laid out in rope, and then run from Llech y Drybedd, at an angle of 53.15° to the '5' side to the present location of the Trefael stone, at a distance of 9610 feet, five times the unit length of the Carningli triangle (to 99.61%). 53.153° is one of the two acute angles in a 3,4,5 Pythagorean triangle.

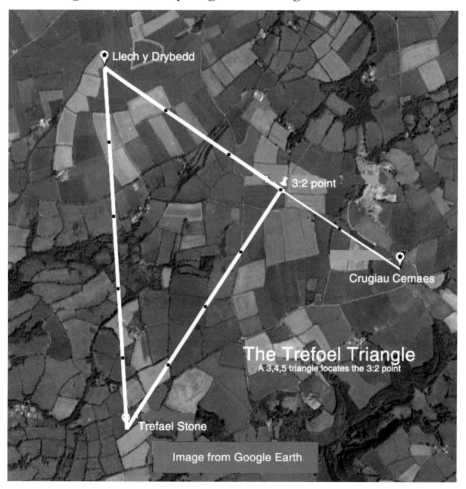

The other acute angle of the 3,4,5 triangle, 36.8° would then then constructed onto the end of this line at Trefael, and taken back to join the '5' side of the Carningli triangle, where it would then *automatically* cut through it at right angles, at the desired 3:2 point. This second line will *automatically* be four units long and where it cuts through the existing '5' side defines three unit lengths from Llech y Drybedd.

Significantly, the 3:2 point lies on a the highest part of a ridge, although without digging there, whatever may have once been marking the spot is now not visible, either having been lost to the plough during subsequent generations of farming by the owners of the nearby farm Trefaes Ganol. Elsewhere on this farm can be found a very large standing stone which, although identified by archaeologists as a cattle rubbing stone, is located equidistant from both Llech y Drybedd and Crugiau Cemaes, as part of a triangular arrangement.

Trefaes Ganol means 'settlement of the middle field' in Welsh. More relevant is that in Old Welsh, *Trefallu* is listed in the dictionary as 'The making of a triangle' which I suppose is the same thing as the more modern word, 'triangulation'. *Trefallu* and *Trefael* are similar words, and one might be forgiven for speculating that the Trefael stone is so named because of some long forgotten ancestral knowledge of its purpose - that it was used in the making of this 3,4,5 triangle from Llech y Drybedd.

Archaeologists may not be able to understand the purpose of all those cup and ring markings on the Trefael stone, but this stone and its location provides the key to understanding an ingenious and elegant geometrical solution to how the 3:2 point on the Carningli triangle was found, and has supplied ample evidence that this technique was applied to achieve that goal. It is, in the context of this book, a likely solution.

A smallish 3,4,5 triangle (or a 5,12,13 triangle) can be pegged out at the end of any line, and its angles replicated and then tracked to sites far away. This is exactly the same method traditionally employed by surveyors when they undertake triangulation. It is most interesting that the megalithic culture in West Wales appears to have been using this geometry in a similar fashion within their surveying of the landscape here, and there will be more to add to this story in a forthcoming work.

Once the crucial 3:2 point had been identified and marked, then the Carningli triangle became a lunation triangle. The 12.369 soli-lunar intermediate hypotenuse could now be measured on the ground, from Carningli summit to the 3:2 point, and given the same treatment as the three sides of the triangle. On page 85, it was measured at 23860.4 ft [*figure obtained via Google Earth*]. This is 8765.76 megalithic yards, which in turn, divided by 8MY (21.776 ft) gives a unitless number 1095.72, and this is immediately recogniseable as the number of days in 3 years.

In lunar months (divide 1095.72 by 29.53059) it delivers 37.1046 lunar months, and there are indeed 37.104 lunar months in 3 years.

The intermediate hypotenuse length thus 'factorises' into three years in units of eight megalithic yards,

3 x 365.2422 = 1095.7 days (which multiplied by 8MY = 23,860.5 feet)

The Carningli triangle is now confirmed to have been constructed as a lunation triangle, a three-year calendar device, using 8MY to represent one day. Astronomy, Geometry and Metrology all confirm the fact.

Scaling between the Stonehenge and Carningli triangles

The scaling factor between the Carningli triangle and that at Stonehenge, within the Station stone rectangle, can now be determined. The unit length of the Stonehenge triangle is eight megalithic yards, or 21.776 feet, while that of the Carningli triangle is 1929.4 feet (using the second method described above). The scaling factor is 1:88.59.

This scaling factor appears to hold no significance whatsoever to a modern scientist who would be more comfortable had it been discovered to be 1:100 or even 1:90. But to a megalithic astronomer, this number would have been entirely familiar, for it is the time period of three lunar months, 88.592 days. [3 x 29.53059 days]

TABLE FIVE
The Scaling factor between the Carningli Triangle and the Station stone Rectangle, from three sets of data.

	Carningli	Stonehenge	Ratio
Longhand	1930.41ft	21.776ft	88.64:1
Google Earth (i)	1928.43ft	21.776ft	88.56:1
Google Earth (ii)	1929.10ft	21.776ft (8MY)	88.59:1

[88.592 days is the astronomical time period for 3 lunar months]

To make the significance of this apparently unconnected scaling factor perfectly clear, the length of the intermediate hypotenuse of the Stonehenge triangle is 269.32557 ft (8 x 2.722 x 12.369 ft). Multiplied by 88.59 this produces the length 23,860 feet, the length of the intermediate hypotenuse of the Carningli triangle, to almost exact precision. The two monuments are connected through their astronomical function, because one day of the three year count (1095.7 days) on the larger triangle has the identical length – eight megalithic yards - as the unit length of the smaller triangle at Stonehenge, an eight year count with a megalithic yard representing a single lunar month.

8 x 1095.7 = 8765.6 MY, which, in feet (multiply by 2.722) is 23,859.96 ft.

For the Carningli triangle the unit length is 12.369 88.59, because,

88.59 x 12.369 = 1095.76 (days)

and the unit length of the Carningli triangle was found to be 1929.1043 ft so that,

1929.1043ft multiplied by 12.369 = 23861 (ft)

and,

1929.1043 ft divided by 88.59 is 21.77ft, which is 8 megalithic yards.

Cultural Connections between West Wales and Stonehenge

Evidence for a cultural connection between the two sites has now been firmly established, the two sites have been shown to be linked through the same synthesis of astronomy, geometry and metrology. This connection is independent of any theories concerning the source of the Stonehenge bluestones, although the material here supports that the bluestones would have been transported to Stonehenge by deliberate human intent.

The lunation triangle needs to be recognised as an important cultural artifact that was employed in Neolithic Britain. The example at Carningli demonstrates the true capabilities of our Neolithic ancestors.

The evidence presented in this chapter reveals the following significant factors concerning the culture or organisation that oversaw this geodetic construction. These are listed below,

1. The Carningli 5,12,13 triangle is a humanly conceived and built construction from around 2850 BC, whose builders already had *a priori* knowledge about the geometric construction that produces a lunation triangle and its properties.

2. The designers made its dimensions astronomically commensurate with day tallying, in this case by using 8 MY as the day count. 1095.7 divisions, each of this length, were measured out along the intermediate hypotenuse in order to represent an exact three solar year count. Each day was therefore represented by a length of 8MY. In comparison, the Stonehenge triangle was

made to represent the 8 year soli-lunar repeat cycle, (8 x 12.369) in units of lunations or lunar months, with one megalithic yard representing the lunar month period (29.53059 days).

3. The 5,12,13 triangle defined by the Station stone rectangle at Stonehenge is commensurate with the Carningli triangle, the scaling being 1:88.59. This scaling ratio directly connects the Stonehenge triangle with the Carningli triangle, because 88.59 days is the time period of three lunar months and this connects the two structures astronomically and metrologically. They were already connected geometrically. A check for the validity of the connection can be made by multiplying the length of the intermediate hypotenuse of the Stonehenge triangle (8 x 2.722 ft x 12.369) which gives 269.35 ft. This same length, 269.32557 ft multiplied by 88.59, gives the length of the intermediate hypotenuse of the Carningli triangle, at 23,861 feet.

Using this integrated technique, an application of megalithic science, the Carningli triangle has revealed the cultural link it shares with Stonehenge, injecting potent new evidence into the current debate concerning the source of the bluestones. The link between Stonehenge and the Preseli bluestone region is now seen to have been forged through similar geometries being replicated at each location, structures that perform the same astronomical and metrological functions even though of greatly differing sizes. The purpose of these structures, and their legacy, is clearly revealed to have originally been Neolithic repositories of astronomical, geometrical and metrological wisdom.

4. The 'thirteen' side of the Carningli triangle, between Carningli and Crugiau Cemaes, is angled up relative to an east-west line such that it forms the hypotenuse of a geodetic 3, 4, 5 triangle whose right angle completes this triangle and is found, appropriately enough at Crosswell, a small hamlet near Pont Saeson, where recently a team of archaeologists lead by Mike Parker Pearson unearthed a rhyolite stone with matching petrology to one found at Stonehenge. There are other very large standing stones arrayed around the point of the right angle, on an adjacent farm called Ty Llwyd. These examples are the real stuff, ophitic (spotted) bluestones. From this point, the other two corners of this 3:4:5 triangle are visible – Carningli summit and Crugiau Cemaes. This triangle is currently being extensively surveyed, as part of other research work on ancient survey lines within a larger landscape array.

5. The conception and subsequent construction of the Carningli triangle preceded the construction of the Station stone rectangle at Stonehenge. This conclusion provides the only logical chronology. The first and much larger triangle was dimensionally determined by locating three high points on the local landscape surrounding Carningli that fortuitively presented a close approximation to a 5,12,13 triangle. A small amount of adjustment was possible to each 'corner', and subsequently made, in order to refine and adjust the dimensions and angles required to achieve the high accuracy of the finished device. Stonehenge, on the other hand, was built as a more formalised and constrained design, and it was the technology and results of those working in the Preseli region who took their ideas, appropriately scaled down in size, to the future temple that was gradually being constructed on Salisbury Plain and which became Stonehenge.

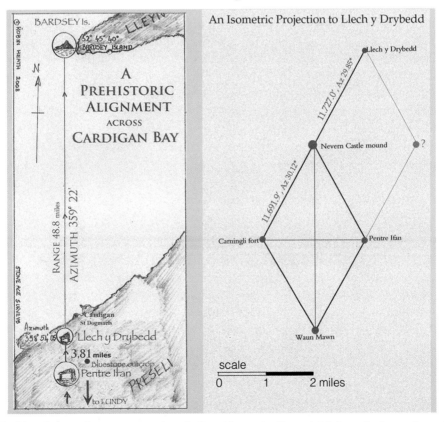

Prehistoric long distance surveying. *Left*, evidence for the establishment of a north-south alignment from Pentre Ifan, Llech y Drybedd and to Bardsey Island. *Right*, an isometric grid whose corners include Pentre Ifan and Llech y Drybedd.

Chapter Seven

Conclusions

This book has told a new story about our ancestors, and provided new and remarkable evidence concerning their capabilities. The evidence suggests that these people once perfected an integrated technology that included astronomy, geometry and metrology and which had been worked out through observing and recording astronomical events, perhaps over many centuries, and storing these as a tally count of days, months and years on lengths of rope and, for shorter lengths of time, on wooden rods.

It appears through the evidence produced here that a system was evolved for storing the astronomical history of a locality within both the megalithic monuments themselves, and also by recording this information onto ropes. Observations made at these monuments could become dated, compared with other observations, and even transferable over long distances, to other observers. By such cooperation, concepts such as latitude would appear to have been understood and then manifested in the choice of location for monuments, the best examples being Stonehenge, Bryn Celli Ddu, on Anglesey, Le Manio and the Crucuno rectangle near Carnac, Brittany. At all of these sites can be found the signatures of the 3,4,5 or the 5,12,13 Pythagorean triangle, within the design of the monument or in its spacial relationships to other nearby monuments.

None of this technology or megalithic science has been picked up by historians, prehistorians or indeed anybody bar a few individuals who work *ex-muris* - outside of any academic institution. This cultural legacy simply has never become part of the story of the history of Britain or northwestern Europe, perhaps because writing in our modern sense of that word never reached these parts until the arrival of the Romans. The lack of conventional forms of writing perhaps sounded the death knell of this cultural tradition, essentially an oral one, in a world that began to record everything using quills and pens onto paper or papyrus which was filled with words and sentences that today make up our history. Despite fragments of this written history suggesting aspects of the older cultural legacy, it has not been appreciated just how evolved the megalithic culture became in solving complex astronomical and navigational problems.

The exposure of some of this evolution surely suggests that megalithic science needs to be included within the curriculum of archaeological training. So much more could be discovered if this component was added to the archaeological toolkit. There is much to be done. We still require to know what was the purpose of creating large geodetic triangles over the landscape of Neolithic Britain. Far larger than would be practicable, these track over formidable terrain where it would be extremely difficult to define accurate measurements. What were these huge geodetic constructions for?

All the astronomy, geometry and metrology involved could have been managed, and the same results achieved, if done on a smaller scale, ideally on a long sandy flat beach or a level stretch of landscape, or even a cursus. All the astronomical work could have been undertaken using wooden posts at the corners of much smaller triangles, without having to build huge megalithic structures such as mounds, dolmens or large standing stones. So what was going on here, both in West Wales and at Stonehenge? Was it all about trying to impress other tribes, or the local chieftain?

These surviving stone structures have been shown to have properties that offer clues. These devices display an underlying expertise in astronomical matters, geometrical surveying and accurate measurement of lengths. The intertwining of counting skills, attained accuracy and astronomical expertise within the same geometry is breathtakingly impressive. This technology and the information it released into the neolithic culture, even within a specialist group within that culture, must have represented an awesome display of power. This knowledge, this megalithic science, was later incorporated into the erection of unfeasibly large stones to create these geometrical arrays, both here and at Stonehenge. It has been said by many archaeologists that Stonehenge, particularly the construction of the later sarsen circle and trilithon ellipse was undertaken mainly to display the huge wealth and power of the Wessex chieftains.

This view may merely be our modern attitudes on such matters being projected back onto the past, but this can hardly be applied to the Carningli triangle, which has remained understated and undetected. Living just a mile from one of its corners and despite actively seeking out such things for over 25 years, I nevertheless failed to 'see' it until 2013. So did everybody else and the triangle remained undetected until then. So I can confidently assert that the Carningli triangle is massively understated, such that its geometry has remained hidden for perhaps over four thousand years.

With the arrival of the Carningli triangle, in 2013, this testament to the Neolithic skill base is seen to be more accurate, much larger, and in many other ways more impressive than that found at Stonehenge. It allows us to see further into the minds of Neolithic 'scientists' and 'engineers', and this is surely a privilege. In seeing into their minds, however briefly, we discover an aspect of our heritage that has been almost completely ignored. These triangles show the human species beginning for the first time to accurately record what was happening in their skies, using a strange technology that is, at the same time, strangely familiar to us today.

In order that future generations can wonder at it all, the Carningli triangle now needs recognition, through further research beyond that of a lone enthusiastic member of the lunatic fringe. It also requires protection, like its smaller cousin on Salisbury Plain. Although the Carningli triangle is situated within the Pembrokeshire National Park, a huge quarry lies within a few hundred metres of the Crugiau Cemaes site. The site itself has been desecrated by allowing a huge concrete reservoir to be built inside it, recently disused and now for sale to the public.

At Llech y Drybedd, during the thirty years I have been visiting this site, things have not been so good for the preservation of this monument. Some visitors light fires inside the dolmen, and New-Age litter can often be found around the site. Grease from the burning of paraffin wax candles has stained the inside of the dolmen. Around 1986, a glass 'tell-tale' was riveted onto a tiny crack in the front orthostat holding up the capstone. It broke within three years and today the glass is long gone, the rivets remain, while the crack has grown to 6-8mm wide. This represents an alarmingly rapid deterioration, a mere blink in the monument's lifetime. Llech y Drybedd urgently needs a little help if its capstone is going to remain standing for a further five millenia.

The Carningli summit is inherently protected simply because of the difficulty of scaling its rocky escarpement. It is why it was chosen as a place to become fortified at some point during prehistory, and why there are the remains of so many hut circles around the summit.

WORLD HERITAGE STATUS

For a site to be included on the World Heritage List, it must meet at least one of the six criteria set out in the UNESCO World Heritage Convention. The Carningli triangle meets three of the six, as set out below:

1. Represents a masterpiece of human creative genius;

2. Exhibits an important interchange of human values, over a span of time or within a cultural area of the world, on developments in monumental arts or town planning or landscape design;

3. Bears a unique or at least exceptional testimony to a cultural tradition or to a civilisation which is living or which has disappeared.

When the megalith building epoch had had its time, around 1600 BC, its cultural tradition truly disappeared and somehow never arrived in our history books. This book reinstates the missing core of that tradition, but it also draws heavily on the work of many other dedicated people, some of whose quotations are woven through the storyline. It seems wholly fitting to finish with two final quotations from two major contributors to our understanding of Stonehenge and the megalithic culture during the last century. The first comes from Richard Atkinson, author of *Stonehenge* and perhaps the last of the great 'gentleman' archaeologists. Here is the final paragraph from his book *Stonehenge*,

'...however much we may be convinced of the superiority of modern methods and modern attitudes to the past, we can be sure that the archaeologists of the future will not hold us blameless. To hope otherwise would be to deny the possibility of further progress, whether at Stonehenge or elsewhere.'

The second quote comes from Alexander Thom, the father of modern archaeoastronomy and the discoverer of megalithic science. Despite the seemingly uncrossable chasm that separated their working methods during the 1960s and 1970s, these two men became close friends and worked together to better understand the purpose of Stonehenge. There is a fine lesson to be learned here.

At the end of the final chapter of *Megalithic Sites in Britain*, Thom wrote,

'Whatever we do we must avoid approaching the study with the idea that Megalithic man was our inferior in ability to think'.

Midsummer sunset at Llech y Drybedd, whose axis of symmetry is aligned to the event. Two small triangular 'windows' enable the sun to shine through the monument as it sets. At this location, Lughnaquilla, a mountain in the WIcklow Hills, Ireland, over ninety miles distant, marked the setting point in 2800 BC. Sometimes the atmospheric conditions enable the mountain to be visible from this site, otherwise the sun sets into the sea horizon.

APPENDIX 1 (page 19 & 40)

CAR-PARK POSTHOLES DATA

The three post holes were surveyed by Thom and Newham and were found to be located at 807.3, 831.3 and 855.5 feet (245, 254 and 260m) from the centre of Stonehenge, and their azimuths from the centre of the monument were measured at 313° 24', 314° 56' and 317° 08' respectively.

APPENDIX 2 (Chapter four)

Further Notes on the Station stone Rectangle

An important consequence of marking the four corners of the rectangle with such large stones, when wooden posts would almost certainly have been used during any laying out of the rectangle on the site, is that it has been easier to assume that the rectangle's corners were laid out onto the perimeter of the Aubrey circle. This turns out not quite to be the case. The holes for the Station stones were dug into the chalk some three centuries after the Aubrey circle was created and measurements of the centres of the present Station stones and the two stone holes places the corners slightly in-board of the Aubrey circle perimeter, only by a small amount, but perhaps significant in confirming the true significance of the rectangle.

For the diagonals of the Station stone rectangle, measurements taken directly from Thom's 1:250 plan reveal the corners to be spaced as follows,

Measured diagonals ('13' sides),
Stone 91 to Stone 93 282 feet 11.67 inches	103.96 MY
Stone 92 to Stone 94 283 feet 9.47 inches	104.25 MY
Average '13' side length	104.1 MY (283.37 feet)

Measured stone to stone dimensions ('12' side)
Stone 92 to Stone 93 260 feet 10.10 inches	95.83 MY
Stone 94 to Stone 91 260 feet 9.92 inches	95.82 MY
Average '12' side dimension	95.825 MY (260.84 feet)

Measured stone to stone dimensions ('5' side)
Stone 91 to Stone 92 110 feet 8.74 inches	40.37 MY
Stone 93 to Stone 94 111 feet 8.72 inches	41.04 MY
Average '5' side dimension	40.20 MY (111.21 feet)

Finding the Unit Length

These measurements offer a way of discovering the unit of length being employed by the constructors of the rectangle. If the perimeters of each of the four possible combinations of 5,12,13 triangle are determined, by summing their individual side lengths, then a division by 30 (5 + 12 + 13) will reveal the best estimate of the unit of length employed in the construction.

91, 92 & 93 8.016 MY
93, 94 & 92, 8.037 MY
91, 92 & 94 8.025 MY
93, 94 & 91 8.027 MY

Average value of unit length **8.026 MY** (within 99.67% of 8MY)
This is an acceptable value of 8 MY for the unit length, better than to 1 part in 200, a realistic tolerance given the size of the rectangle, the present state it is in, and the limitations of using large stones or their postholes instead of ropes or rods to define the corners. These lengths are by no means perfectly matched to their ratios, nor would the tolerance be likely to improve during comparable surveying exercises done today using just ropes, pegs and rulers. They are the kind of figures one might expect from a field surveying exercise undertaken without modern surveying instruments led by an experienced surveyor backed by a well coordinated team.It will probably never be possible to prove that the Station stone rectangle was designed to comprise 5 units (sides), 12 units (sides) and 13 units (diagonals) each of eight megalithic yards. One must recognise that the positions for two of these stones (92 and 94) are based solely on probing and excavating the hole that once held a stone. In addition stone 91 now lies recumbent next to its hole. The best realistic estimates for the centres of three of the four stones will have a tolerance of ±15 cms (or ±6 inches).

However much the finer details of the rectangle are discussed, now or *ad nauseum* into the future, it is probably never going to be possible to establish the exact original positions for three of the four stones. Atkinson offers us all a way out of this dull and fruitless debate in his earlier quotation; the original laying out of the rectangle would have been done with markers, probably wooden posts, and the four stones would have been sunk into the chalk later, as a more enduring 'symbolic' representation of the intent of that original survey.

APPENDIX 3 (Chapter 4, pages 19-27)
Locating the Centre of the Aubrey Circle

The assumption that a 5:12 rectangle was intended leads to some more positive inquiry. It makes one think about what was being undertaken at Stonehenge. For example, after the three centuries or so following the Aubrey circle of holes having been back-filled, these 56 holes would effectively have been reclaimed by the chalk downland, and much less distinct. Establishing the centre of this circle, especially one in this state, would have been no simple matter. And that centre must be accurately located prior to defining an accurate rectangular form on the perimeter of the Aubrey circle. Its diagonals would have to be equal if that form is to be 'square-on', and these must each pass right through the centre of the circle.

The builders could have employed any rectangular shape to redefine the centre of the Aubrey circle, but they employed a 5:12 rectangle. Not only that, but they arranged it such that its shorter sides aligned to the midsummer sunrise in or around 2700 BC, and by intent or by coincidence, they arranged for the longer sides to align such that their northwestern ends pointed to the horizon position of the most northerly moonset at the moon's major standstill every 18.6 years, in 2700 BC. The original axis of the monument also formed part of this arrangement.

So it is seen to be not true that the rectangle was solely a geometrical way for re-establishing the lost centre of the Aubrey circle. The Station stone rectangle was an astronomically, geometrically and metrologically integrated construction. It could not have employed the original Aubrey holes, for these were not suitably spaced to mark the four points of the 5:12 rectangle. The Aubrey holes were, despite their accurate radial spacing, not regularly spaced sufficiently well around the perimeter to allow a square or rectangular structure to be erected with sufficient accuracy.

It can be safely assumed that the Station stone rectangle was an attempt to improve or adapt the original structure, which before around 2700 BC consisted of the ditch and bank, the Aubrey circle, the entrance causeway and the heel stone. The 'ideal' metrology for the monument, the goal one assumes the builders were aiming for, was to make the rectangle's side lengths 40 x 96 MY, making the diagonals 104 MY. The builders achieved an average tolerance error of better than 1 part in 200, which is 1.4 ft in 283.6 feet, close enough to indicate the intentions of the builders.

The small fractional component of each dimension in MY given in the figures given on page 98 supports that the 8 MY unit was intentional. The presumption can now be made that whoever located the holes into which the Station stones were dropped knew all about 5,12,13 triangles and was designing this early part of the Stonehenge infrastructure using 8 MY as the rectangle's unit of length. This is a logical conclusion based on dimensions supplied through objective data obtained from Thom's theodolite 'closed' survey, which is self-checking. I have personally run marked ropes across from stone 93 to the supposed position of the hole that once marked stone 92, and that rope measured just under 96 MY. From the recumbent stone base (stone 91) to the supposed position of stone 94 measured 96.10 MY.

The measurement of shape and length in a geometrical structure thus reveals crucial information enabling the accuracy of the geometry to be assessed. From this first simple step has followed an insight into the abilities and intent of the architects and constructors of the monument in question. Even an order of procedure during its construction could be suggested, beyond the scope of this present work.

APPENDIX 4 (page 5)

The Astronomic Significance of the Megalithic yard.

Unlikely as it may at first appear, there is a significant astronomical relationship between Megalithic yard and the foot measure. The ratio of the length of the foot to that of the megalithic yard is almost identical to that of the difference between the solar year and the lunar year, in days (twelve lunar synodic months) and the length of the lunar month, in days.

1. As lengths of time,
   Solar year minus lunar year, $365.2422 - 354.367 = 10.875$ days
   The lunar (Synodic) month $= 29.53059$ days
   The ratio $10.875 : 29.53059$ normalises to $1:2.7154$

Expressed in feet, this is 1 foot : 2.7154 feet. In inches it is 12 : 32.585
The fractional component, 0.368 lunar months, is one English foot (to 1 part in 2,375), almost exactly expressed by the fraction 7/19 MY. The foot forms the ratio 1:2.7154 compared to the lunar month period. I have termed this length, expressed in feet, the *astronomical megalithic yard* (AMY), 2.7154 feet, or 32.585 inches. The fraction 7/19 I have previously called the *silver fraction*.

Metrologically, 2.7154 feet is the step formed from 2.5 root canonical Belgic Feet (from J F Neal, *Measuring the Megaliths*, Secret Academy, 2007)

In astronomical terms, there are 12.368267 lunar months in one solar year. Expressed or represented in astronomical megalithic yards, this becomes represented as a length of 33.585 feet, which is 12 lunar months (12 AMY = 32.585 feet) plus the fraction of a month (one foot), totalling 33.585 feet.

The Metrological Significance of the Megalithic Yard

2. As lengths, the metrological megalithic yard (MMY)
            One Foot : One Megalithic yard = 1:2.722

It is clear from the above that the Megalithic yard can be considered a measure of length that corresponds to the lunar month, a fundamental measure of time.

Metrologically, this length of the AMY is the step formed from 2.5 standard canonical Belgic feet. These two lengths, the AMY and the metrological MY are connected through the ratio 440 : 441 to each other. This ratio in ancient metrology is the traditional ratio for the polar radius and that of the mean radius of the earth.
            Earth's polar radius 3949.7142 miles
            Earth's mean radius 3958. 6909 miles

APPENDIX 5 (page 10)

Perhaps most importantly, a message went out from Clive Ruggles that evidence from these sources was no longer worthy of attention. Indeed, on the brochure for the course given out by the School of Archaeology and Ancient History at Leicester one could read, incredibly,

'Thom's "megalithic astronomy". In the course we do not consider the work of Alexander Thom and its reassessment in any detail, partly because the subject is a very technical one and partly because many of the issues are no longer of archaeological interest.'

This wholly unnecessary put down, aimed at the founder of the same subject of which he now held the Chair, was made by the same man who, during his inauguration to the Chair of Archaeoastronomy, had also said, rather confusingly,

'...the technical concepts underlying a great deal of archaeoastronomy are really very simple'.

A quotation from Gavin Lucas's book *The Archaeology of Time (Routledge, 2005)* eloquently sums up the traditional view of archaeologists on megalithic science and the subject matter in this book,

> *'Indeed, it is only really when archaeology leaves the realm of trying to recover evidence of time-reckoning and explores more general issues of temporal perception in the past and its relation to social practice that the most rewarding studies are to be found.'*

Lucas was, at the time of publication of his book, the Assistant Director of the Institute of Archaeology in Reykjavik. Perhaps we should offer a quote in reply,

> *'Any inquiry into the past which does not reckon with the dimension of time is obviously nonsense'*

Stuart Piggott, Approach to Archaeology, Penguin, 1959

APPENDIX 6 (page 54)

Repeat Calendar Cycles of the Sun and Moon

Knowledge of the cycles of the sun and moon is woefully inadequate within our modern urban population. The motions of the sun and moon are no longer taught in any depth in schools. This regrettable situation has made it difficult for many people to assess data concerning astronomical alignments obtained from archaeological sites. Such work is sometimes seen to complicate what is universally experienced as a beautiful, natural and observable phenomenon – watching the rising or setting of sun or moon over a distant horizon. Being informed on the astronomy of this phenomenon is hardly going to diminish that experience, and can only enhance consciousness of what is actually going on.

Viewed from a megalithic site designed to record a solstitial or equinoctial sun on a certain date and which can provide the length of the year to within a few minutes connects the observer directly to the same cosmic rhythms that orchestrate the dance of life of earth. Yet despite their cultural importance, solar and lunar alignments are hardly mentioned in UK archaeology. It was most unfortunate that the matter of prehistoric alignments was ever placed into their charge in the first place, it was never a welcome addition to their perception of prehistory, and perhaps it might better belong in the more welcoming hands of those that study the history of science.

APPENDIX 7 (page 35)
Alan Penny's Discovery
Heelstone to Centre 260.8333 ft

Longer sides of Station stones

91-94 & 92-93 = 3125" = 260.416 ft

Aubrey diameter	92-94	= 3400"	= 283.3 ft	104.47 MY
	91-93	= 3387.5"	= 282.292 ft	103.7 MY
	1-28	= 3437.5"	= 286.45 ft	105.23 MY

APPENDIX 8 (page 27)
Thom, Stonehenge and Avebury Surveys

Alexander Thom, for two decades the Head of engineering at Oxford, was well qualified to deal with the matter of detecting if a fixed unit of length had been applied in the construction of megalithic sites. He had spent more time than anyone else investigating the matter. Following the three month long survey of Avebury ring in the 1960s, Thom found that 2.722 feet was the value of one unit of length frequently employed throughout Britain and Brittany in the construction of megalithic monuments. He had previously, in 1967, called this unit the Megalithic yard (MY), and defined its length as 2.72 ft ± 0.003 feet.] Employing this unit to measure the 5:12 rectangle at Stonehenge reveals that the sides are 95.74 and 40.23 megalithic yards (MY). The two diagonals are both diameters of the Aubrey circle, and these become 104.26 MY.

It is important to investigate sites with a full awareness that astronomy or time cycles will often be linked to measurements at the site. Various units of length appear to have been employed, the main ones being the inch (day) and the megalithic yard (the lunar month), although the inch is also employed, as at Le Manio. One good example of the use of inches at Stonehenge is found in the diameter of the Aubrey circle.

The Aubrey soli-lunar calendar (see page 31) track the rotation of the lunar nodes within their 18.6 year cycle. After half a cycle, when the nodes have made half a revolution, the eclipse seasons occur at the same times of the year, across a diameter of the Aubrey circle, after 3400 days. The Aubrey circle diameter is 283.6 feet (Thom survey), which is 3403 inches.

Avebury

Seventeen miles north of Stonehenge is a second henge temple, the largest known, at Avebury. Thom's survey in the mid 1960s showed that the geometry of the outer ring of stones, which once contained between 98 and 100 huge sarsen stones, was determined from three points, each a corner of a single 3,4,5 triangle located in the middle of the henge. Long radius arcs were struck from each of the triangle's corners.

   If 99 stones were placed in the perimeter ring, then Avebury could have been another type of eight year calendar. The perimeter was measured by Thom at 1302.5 megalithic yards, which is 3543.67 feet, almost exactly ten times the lunar year expressed in days, to 99.95%, or 1 part in 200. The lack of clarity over the total number of stones is regrettable, a sad outcome from the vandalism that this site suffered in recent centuries. Atkinson and Piggot claimed 100 stones, Thom had 98 or 99 and the National Trust claim 98, Various other sources state 98 or 99 stones.

APPENDIX 9
(Avebury Factoids)

1. Avebury is the largest known stone circle *anywhere*.

2. The surrounding ditch and bank is 2/3rds mile in circumference.

3. The *most* accurate survey was undertaken between by Professor Alexander Thom in 1978.

4. Thom reported that the perimeter of the outer stone ring was 1302.5 Megalithic yards (MY) of 2.722 feet, which is 3545.4 feet or 520 Megalithic rods (1 MR = 2.5 MY).

5. The geometry of the ring is based on a circle 200MY in radius with centre at point D, exactly 60 MY from C (see diagram opposite).

6. A 3-4-5 pythagorean triangle ABC of side lengths 30-40-50 MR (75, 100 and 125 MY) defined the geometry. From the corners of this triangle (stones/markers have long gone) the various arcs that make up the outer ring were struck. Their radii and arc lengths are as follows: from A,B and C, each radius 260 MY, define arc FG, length 200 MY, arc HG, length 130 MY, and arc ML, length 200 MY respectively. In addition, there were two longer arcs struck from outside of the ring of length 750 MY, from point W and Z (*see skyandlandscape.com*).

7. The two inner circles are each 125 MY in radius and are therefore as big as any other true circle known in Britain, and the same size as the massive Ring of Brogar in the Orkneys.

8. Avebury, unlike nearly all other stone rings, has CORNERS, which define the arc lengths. Thom showed that all the arc lengths are integral in Megalithic rods.

9. Avebury is a MESS. The ring was heavily vandalised in history, has a village built within and without it, and a major road system has quartered it. Most of the stones were fallen or missing in 1930. Despite this, Alexander Keiller and other archaeologists were able to locate the vast majority of the stone holes in the chalk and the integrity of the geometry of the original ring has since been established.

APPENDIX 10 (*page 71*)

The St David's Alignment

The 'throne' on Carningli summit provides the observing point for a spectacular solar alignment. On February 18th (and October 24th), the sun is seen to set into the 'egg cup' or 'grail' provided by two of larger outcrops (hardly are they mountains) near St Davids, Carn Llidi (*on the left*) and Penberi (*on the right*). From this position, the two outcrops form the perfect concave shape to receive the sun as it sets, but only on this particular pair of dates during the year.

Between Carn Ingli summit and the two outcrops stands Carn Briw, directing the observer where to look to watch this event. From the 'sharp end' of the Carningli triangle it is therefore easily possible to confirm that any calendar is tracking with seasons, and I have observed the February event on more than eight sunny occasions in order to observe the extra quarter day 'creep' across the two outcrops, a 'creep' that reverts back to year zero position every four years, and has added an extra day in the process, after 1461 sunsets have elapsed.

1461 day counts on a rope, then folded into four, reveals 365.25 days as the length of the seasonal year, as accurate as our modern calendar.

More on this alignment is available from *Bluestone Magic (Bluestone Press, 2010)*, which has the benefit of colour photographs.

APPENDIX 11 - SITE COORDINATES
GPS and OS MAP Coordinate data
(Angles given in DD.DDDD format, elevations given in Feet)
Geoid is OSGB36 format.
To convert these coordinates to WGS84 (which Google Earth uses) a conversion website will need to be used. There are many to choose from.

Pentre Ifan N 51.99865 ; W4.768833 ; El 496'
Mount Leinster N 52.61666 ; W6.73333 ; El 2610'
Ramsey Is. Alignment N 51.86236 ; W5.338467 ; El 320'
Mount Leinster N 52.61666 ; W6.73333 ; El 2610
Long Meg orthostat N 54.72748 ; W2.6668 ; El 552'
Helvellyn summit N 54.52222 ; W3.0000 ; El 3118'
Barclodiad y Gawres N 53.20698 ; W4.502806 ; El 40'
Holy Island (Môn) trig pt. N 53.3129 ; W4.674417 ; El 722'
Nine Maidens row southern term N 50.47085 ; W4.90845 ; El 579'
Nine Maidens row northern term N 50.47173 ; W4.907784 ; El 648.5' (Az 25.72773)
St Michael's Mount N 50.12 ; W5.47639 ; El 400'
Tintagel Head N 50.66806 ; W4.7625 ; El 579' - 240'
Bardsey Is peak N 52.761111 ; W4.780556 ; El 548'
Arbor Low N 53.168889 ; W1.761667 ; El ?
Bryn Celli Ddu N 53.207706 ; W4.234722 ; El ?
Frenni Fawr trig pt. N 51.98318 ; W4.61715 ; El 1300'
Llech y Drybedd N 52.05417 ; W4.77037 ; El 612'
Lugnaquilla summit N 52.95000 ; W6.41667 ; El 1809'
Crug Cemaes trig pt N 52.04073 ; W1.4.73362 ; El 646'
Carn Enoch peak N 51.99557 ; W4,896266 ; El 969'
Carn Briw tip N 51.99762 ; W4.8316 ; 1119'
Dinas Is trig pt N 52.03276 ; W4.90833 ; El 466'
Carreg y Gof N 52.01335 ; W4.861483; El 189'
Carreg y Gof cupstone N 52.01353 ; W 4.9127 ; 162'
Parc y Meirw N51.98545 ; W4.914133 ; El 527'
Penrhiw chamber N52.01152 ; W4.99875 ; El 447'
Carn Wen TP N51.9241 ; W 4.6655833
Preseli Stonehenge Lunation triangle (Apex) N51.922314 ; W 4.6710556
Nevern Cross N52.025 ' W 4.7937833 (GPS 30' east)
Nevern Castle (mossy mound) N 52.026367 ' W 4.7951667
Nevern Castle (tower mound) N 52.02630 ; W 4.7964833 (204')
Foel Feddau Cairn N 51.956917 ' W 4.7622167 (1527')
Vesica 'Waun Maun' N 51.97055 ' W4.7950167
Twin stones near 'Waun Maun' N 51.968167 ' W 4.7932833
Cwnc yr Hydd Square XS stone N 51.971333 ' W 4.7899667
Cwnc yr Hydd recumbent N 51.971267 ' W 4.7897833 (points to bluestone site)
Cwnc yr Hydd recumbent N 51.97135 ; W 4.790333 (Fishguard end)
King Arthur's Hall, Bodmin SW corner N 50.567883 ; 4.6414167 (847')
Trellyfiant Stone N 52.04562 ; W 4.79575 (El ~475')
Waun Mawn N 51.97055 ; W 4.795017 (El 968')
Trellyfiant N 52.047483 ; W 4.797 (El 495')

APPENDIX TWELVE
(Table One and pages 81 & 82)

The azimuth of the extreme northerly minor moonset from Crugiau Cemaes is the same as the angle of the '5' side of the Carningli triangle. The moon would be seen to touch the horizon directly behind Llech y Drybedd and this would occur for a few months every 18.6 years. Another local site, Y Gaer, operates in the same way to mark the major standstill moonset, again by using Llech y Drybedd's capstone as the foresight *(see skyandlandscape website for PDF report).*

It is hard to consider the angle of the '5' side of the Carningli triangle not being chosen due to the alignment to the minor moonset, which was exact *prior* to 3000 BC.

STONE AGE SURVEYS
THIS IS QUICKAZ, FINDS AZIMUTHS IN A FLASH!

This calculation is for azimuth of Minor Moonset(e-i) at Crugiau Cemaes in 3000 BC.

The proposed moonset is in the NW quadrant.
Epoch 3000BC (e = 24.03*)
Declination = 18.88477*
Latitude = 52.05*
Horizon Altitude = 0*
Correction for Earth's Curvature = .0144*
Parallax Correction = .95*
Refraction Correction = 0.6*
Cos Azimuth = .5243937 . Apparent Altitude = 8.559997E-02
                          ^   ^   ^
                              ^   ^   ^
********- horizon -****************^****^****^***********
Disc on Horizon =   300.5083 degrees
Disc half set =   301.2523 degrees
Last Flash =   301.6274 degrees
Azimuth of Llech y Drybedd from Crugiau Cemaes
trig. point is **300.516** degrees, within half a minute of
one degree of the moon touching the horizon.
****
Program by Robin Heath, Stone Age Surveys, 2014

APPENDIX THIRTEEN
(Using astronomy to date archaeological sites)

Dating a site through astronomical measurements is not a new technique, and it cannot always provide the accuracy that is required by archaeologists. In this case, with the distance between the foresight and backsight being nearly two miles, and with both sites at the same height above sea level, we have the chance to obtain results that confidently suggest a date prior to 3000BC for the establishment of the azimuth. As the Carningli triangle utilises this alignment as its '5' side, it would follow that the triangle is of this period. By 2500 BC, the azimuth of the minor moonset would have changed to 300.42 degrees, nearly a tenth of one degree. The moon's disc would have visibly moved to the left, by a sixth of its own diameter. The '5' side is clearly not at this angle, hence the best estimate for its inception would be around 3000 BC, placing it a few centuries before the supposed construction of the Station stone rectangle, i.e. the Carningli triangle preceded this stage of Stonehenge. The dates and corresponding azimuths of the minor moonset viewed from Crugiau Cemaes are, in degrees,

Date	Azimuth
3500 BC	300.58
3000 BC	300.50
2800 BC	300.45
2500 BC	300.42

The coming of age of a journey

Index

111

Printed by Gomer Press, Llandysul